World of the Founders

Cover: *James Caldwell's riverside manufactory near the northern boundary of the city of Albany. From the collection of the New York State Museum, Albany.*

World of the Founders:
New York Communities
in the Federal Period

Edited by Stephen L. Schechter
& Wendell Tripp

New York State Commission on the Bicentennial of the
United States Constitution • Albany, New York • 1990

The New York State Commission on the Bicentennial
of the United States Constitution, Albany, New York

Library of Congress Cataloging in Publication Data
World of the Founders: New York Communities in the Federal Period
    Edited by Stephen L. Schechter and Wendell Tripp
    1. New York (State)—History—1775–1865. 2. New York (State)—Social life
and customs. I. Schechter, Stephen L., 1945– . II. Tripp, Wendell, III. New
York State Commission on the Bicentennial of the United States Constitution.
F123.W67 1990   89-9238
974.7'03—dc20   CIP

ISBN 0-945660-02-2

Manufactured in the United States of America

Contents

Contributors

Stefan Bielinski is director of the Colonial Albany Social History Project and the author of a number of essays on the history of colonial New York. He has edited several bibliographies of New York State sources and is the author of monographs on Abraham Yates, Jr., Frederick Philipse, and the Dongan Charter of 1686.

Kenneth R. Bowling, associated with the First Federal Congress Project at George Washington University, Washington, D.C., is associate editor of *The Documentary History of the First Federal Congress,* co-editor of volume 9, *The Diary of William Maclay and other Notes on Senate Debates* (1988), and is the author of *The Creation of Washington, D.C., The Idea and Location of an American Capital* (George Mason University Press, 1990).

Leo Hershkowitz, of the Department of History at Queens College of the City University of New York, is the author or editor of monographs ranging from the eighteenth-century letters of the Franks family to *Tweed's New York: Another Look* (Doubleday, 1977), and has written articles on aspects of New York's social and legal history.

Jacob Judd is a member of the Department of History at Lehman College and the Graduate Center of the City University of New York. He is the author of articles and of several monographs relating to life in the Hudson Valley in the colonial and early national periods, and has edited document collections and anthologies on New York colonial and economic history.

Jessica Kross, a member of the Department of History at the University of South Carolina, is the author of *The Evolution of an American Town* (Temple University Press, 1983) and of a number of articles and papers on American colonial history and historiography.

William Siles is Historian at the Strong Museum in Rochester, New York. He has published several articles and scholarly papers on aspects of social and economic life in central New York, and has also written museum studies relating to life and work in the Genesee Country.

Editors' Introduction

A mere handful of individuals were involved in the central events that marked the creation of the government of the United States. The Declaration of Independence had but fifty-six signers, the Constitution but thirty-nine. And even if the delegates to the several state conventions that ratified the Constitution are included, the total number remains relatively small. Historians and political scientists have subjected these events and many of their participants to microscopic examination in scores of monographs and hundreds of articles. And rightfully so, for the events, though few, and the numbers involved, though small, form eternal landmarks in the history of our nation.

The present volume, however, has a different focus. Confining itself to the New York State scene, it presents a broad yet detailed survey of community development in an age of nation-building. Specifically, it presents descriptive and analytical examinations of five New York State communities during the federal period—the years when an effective national government was accepted by the people of New York State.

The communities selected cover a broad geographical expanse —from western Long Island to New York City, through the Hudson Valley to Albany, thence westward to the frontier region that centered upon the farthest of the Finger Lakes. These studies, taken altogether, also range through a broad period of time. Though their central events are those of the federal period, the demands of context and logical exposition compel the inclusion, in some studies, of material relating to the Revolution and, in others, of material that carries the story into the nineteenth century. Though no one of the authors explicitly makes the claim, it may be concluded that these communities unfold not within a series of historical segments labelled Revolution, Confederation, Constitution, but within a single period of development in which a colonial people cast off one set of governmental garments and tried on a couple of others before attaining a fit that was acceptable, if not immediately comfortable.

These studies, in any case, illuminate the activities of men and women in specific New York State locales during several formative decades in the history of the state and nation. These men and women were, without question, affected by the grand events of their day, but in each of these studies the author emphasizes the local reaction to events, and it is this that marks the contribution of each study.

Jessica Kross presents a detailed analysis of the small town of Newtown, in Queens County, which endured seven years of British occupation and underwent physical, demographic, and economic change in the thirteen years that followed the British departure. The strength of Kross's study is in its demographic and statistical analysis, which, leavened with anecdotal vignettes, reveals the changing patterns of community life while concluding that the village of 1777 was still recognizable in 1800.

Studies of New York City by Kenneth Bowling and by Leo Hershkowitz concentrate on the years when the city was the nation's first seat of government under the Constitution. Less given to statistical analysis than Kross, Bowling and Hershkowitz nevertheless provide extraordinary detail about daily life in New York during the federal period, while also providing graphic descriptions of the changes that took place in the physical character of the small city and in its inhabitants. Devastated by seven years of British occupation, the city enjoyed sound leadership as it rebuilt itself and became the home of Congress under the Articles of Confederation, 1785–1788, and then the seat of the new federal government in 1789. The two studies form, in a sense, the centerpiece of the volume because they deal with the state's largest community and with a center of widely influential events. At the same time, theirs are community studies that bridge the interests of the political scientist and the social historian. As Hershkowitz focuses on the hosts, Bowling focuses on the guests, to present in tandem a word portrait of the cultural, economic, political, and social dimensions of the first federal city and of the "Republican Court" that made it preeminent.

Moving the volume's focus north of Manhattan Island into the lower Hudson Valley, Jacob Judd examines the evolving relationship between tenants and manor lords in Westchester County, from the eve of the Revolution into the 1780s. He thus examines a community that is defined less by geographical space than by an ongoing dialogue between two groups whose traditional relationship changed gradually over time and then rapidly as Revolution and Independence transformed colonial Westchester into a vigorous segment of a new state in a new nation.

Farther north, located at the head of navigation on the Hudson River, Albany was New York State's second city. Stefan Bielinski breaks new ground in his study of this crossroads city—at a site where the axis of routes north and south bisected the most efficient westerly route—as he details the development of a community that came of age during the federal period. Exploiting the wealth of material compiled by the Colonial Albany Social History Project, Bielinski describes the physical transformation of the city, the profound changes in the composition of the population, and especially the commercial and industrial changes that influenced Albany's transformation during these years into an urban center, a bustling gateway to the west, and the seat of the state's government.

William Siles completes the survey and the journey with a study of communities on the fringe of settlement in the western reaches of New York's Finger Lakes region. He describes the process of acquisition, survey, and settlement of the lands, with Oliver Phelps of the Commonwealth of Massachusetts as the chief protagonist, and the creation of village communities, Canandaigua in particular, as the focal activity. Siles's intense examination reveals that while the inhabitants of western New York lived on the frontier of settlement, a great distance from the older inhabited regions of the state, they did not for long live in a wilderness. He shows in great detail how they rapidly tranformed that vast unsettled tract into a prospering community that replicated the older settled region to the east. In doing this, he deals with all aspects of the process—economics, politics, culture, religion, social life, city-building.

The end result of this six-part effort is a composite of community life and community development in the years when great dramatic events took place on the national stage. The strength of the total effort is in the variety of localities examined —each at a different level of development, at a varying distance from centers of events, subject to different geographical influences, subject in varying degrees to the wishes of governmental bodies. Purposefully kaleidoscopic in the number and variety of their views of community life, the essays also have a theme in common: While some of the communities, notably Newtown, tended to be inward-looking and self-contained, and others, notably New York City, were outward-looking and broadly influential, all were in ferment, all were enduring a process of change. Yet all retained, even as they were transformed, a core of characteristics that were rooted in the past. These were years of drastic change, of growth and transformation, but the rush of events could not erase completely the ancient elements of community life in New York State.

World of the Founders

City Hall, on Wall Street, as it appeared before it was enlarged and redecorated for the use of the First Federal Congress. Courtesy of the New-York Historical Society.

New York City, Capital of the United States, 1785–1790

Kenneth R. Bowling

New York City received a splendid Christmas gift from the United States government in 1784 when the Confederation Congress chose it as its place of residence until a permanent seat of government could be built. In 1790, Congress moved to Philadelphia. New York City was the federal capital for only five and one-half years; nevertheless, the relationship proved fruitful for both the United States and New York City. The federal government's presence profoundly influenced the recovery of the country's most war-devastated city, and New York, in return, provided Congress with a pleasant, largely problem-free seat. In addition, the social conventions of the federal government during its first decade took root at New York. The "Republican Court," though it would precisely mirror the British Court, nevertheless reflected the British aura of its host.[1]

In 1774 some Americans had argued that the First Continental Congress should convene in New York, but instead it met and remained at Philadelphia, except when the British army forced it to flee. Its tenure there was not always comfortable and congressmen frequently complained about local interference in federal affairs. In June of 1783, after a jurisdictional confrontation with Pennsylvania, the most serious of several which had occurred over the previous decade, Congress moved the legislative functions of the federal government to Princeton,

1

New Jersey. During the next year and a half it also met in Annapolis, Maryland, and Trenton, New Jersey. Philadelphia's supporters regularly attempted to bring Congress "home," but op-
ponents, centered in New England, refused. In the fall of 1784
when the New York legislature invited Congress to New York
City, dislike of Philadelphia, a longing for the accommodations
and services available only in cities, and the desire to provide
stability for the federal government led Congress to accept the
invitation.[2]

Congress convened in New York City in January 1785. The
city and its 20,000-some residents had not yet recovered from
a seven-year occupation by the British Army, two major fires,
and the loss of half of its population and commerce. Its selection as the seat of federal government promised revitalization,
and New Yorkers welcomed Congress accordingly. City officials
and private citizens spent two hectic weeks preparing. Ecstatic
New Yorkers greeted the body with lavish addresses, a thirteen-
gun salute from the Battery, and a banquet attended by city
and state officials as well as the diplomatic corps. A newspaper
editorial declared the event to be of such magnitude to the city
as to give New York a great name among nations.

Delegates found ample accommodations, the city provided
Congress with part of City Hall for its use, and Congress rented
space at Fraunces Tavern for the departments of foreign affairs
and war. New Yorkers began to reestablish the city's social life,
with Congress at its center. Sumptuous dinners, crowds of invitations, and a frenzy of visits kept the members entertained during the early weeks of 1785. By the end of the year, elegant
private parties, fortnightly concerts, and theater three nights
a week provided entertainment. So many congressmen married
New York women that one delegate dubbed Manhattan "Cal-
ypso's Island." Accustomed to criticizing Philadelphia and the
towns in which Congress had previously resided, members made
almost no complaint against New York. They described its
citizens as the most hospitable people imaginable. Even Philadelphia partisans like Hannah Thomson, wife of Secretary of
Congress Charles Thomson and first lady of the federal government in the absence of the wife of the president of Congress,
admitted to the city's agreeableness.

The years 1785–1788 witnessed the revitalization of the federal government. The local concerns and jurisdictional conflicts that so distracted Congress during the Philadelphia years, did not occur at New York. Congress reunited the executive and legislative functions of the federal government. Those who argued that they could better serve in Philadelphia were asked to resign. Such significant and long-term accomplishments as the land ordinances of 1785 and 1787 highlight the accomplishments of the Confederation Congress during its New York years. Southerners nevertheless objected to the special influences of the North upon a Congress that resided so far from the center of the Union. Beginning in 1787, they joined the Pennsylvanians in attempts to return Congress to Philadelphia. They almost succeeded in April 1787, arguing that Congress should be there to keep an eye on the Constitutional Convention, scheduled to meet in May.[3]

On July 2, 1788, the twelfth anniversary of the day that Congress had declared the colonies independent states, a ten-gun salute blasted many New Yorkers awake at 5 A.M.: Virginia had become the tenth state to ratify the proposed Constitution. Although the Constitution was put into effect when the ninth state, New Hampshire, ratified it, Virginia was a powerful and highly Antifederal state. When Virginia ratified, Antifederalist New Yorkers lost their strongest ally. Bells rang for four hours. Many Yorkers devoted the day to amusement. Two days later, Antifederalists burned the Constitution at a ceremony on the Battery. Altercations with Federalists followed.

Congress began the process for convening the new federal government on July 2, but it then postponed debate. The postponement put additional pressure on the New York State ratifying convention then meeting at Poughkeepsie: ratify the Constitution and the First Federal Congress could be convened at New York; defeat it and New York City would no longer be the seat of federal government. Samuel Osgood, perhaps the most socially prominent opponent of the Constitution in New York City, informed Antifederalists at the Poughkeepsie convention that the universal opinion in the city was that New York State's vote on the Constitution and the seat of the First Federal Congress had become intimately connected. The strongly Federalist city was therefore especially fierce in its opposition to Governor George Clinton and the Antifederalists since defeat for the Constitution meant that Congress, with all its attendant benefits, would be forced to leave. This tension, which was of course unique to the ratification struggle in New York City, undoubtedly contributed to the unusual violence in New York City during July 1788.

At the Poughkeepsie convention, fear of New York City's losing its status as the seat of federal government provided common ground for the leading spokesmen on both sides, all of whom, except Clinton, represented that part of the state lying east of the Hudson and south of Poughkeepsie. The resulting compromise delivered enough downstate Antifederalist votes to ratify the Constitution and a Federalist endorsement of a circular letter to the states calling for a second federal convention to amend it. When the news reached New York at 9 P.M. on Saturday evening, July 26, the city exploded. Bells rang, cannons fired, New Yorkers drank in the streets, and, after midnight, an intoxicated mob attacked the offices of the Antifederalist *New York Journal.* Congressman James Madison informed George Washington that the question of ratification in New York had become bound up with the city's continued status as the seat of federal government and condemned Alexander Hamilton, John Jay, and other New York City Federalists for agreeing to the dangerous circular letter. He could attribute it only to the willingness of New Yorkers to do anything to retain Congress.

On Monday, Congress again considered the steps involved in convening the new government. Delegates knew that they faced a major sectional battle on the question of where the First Congress should meet, but no one expected to spend six difficult weeks reaching a decision. The French consul considered the debate one of the most passionate in congressional history. While it raged, Philadelphians filled their newspapers with attacks on New York. The serious criticisms were that its location in the Union was too far north; its public buildings inadequate and badly situated; and its harbor an open invitation to enemy navies. Philadelphia could properly boast of a central location, magnificent accommodations, and a less exposed harbor, but it suffered from other comparisons with New York. Despite a rise in crime—including robbery and murder—mob violence in 1788 related to ratification and to the medical community's practice of graverobbing for purposes of dissection, and a jurisdictional dispute between New York City and the

Dutch minister involving diplomatic immunity, few people suggested that New York provided the kind of unfit environment characteristic of Philadelphia—according to that city's enemies. New York City's advocates in Congress argued on its behalf the cost of transferring federal functions to another site and the possibility of a return to the instablity which had plagued Congress in 1783 and 1784. Most importantly, they claimed that Congress had implied its intention to remain at New York City if the state ratified the Constitution. Hamilton allegedly told Congress that New York's congressional delegation had assured the state ratifying convention that this would be the case.

By late August 1788, Federalists throughout the United States began to worry that implementation of the Constitution was threatened by the struggle. Finally, even the Philadelphians gave up. "Let the place of meeting be New York" or even "the banks of the Potomac, Ohio, or Mississippi, let it be anywhere; but for Heaven's sake . . . let the government be put in motion." On September 13, after two state delegations had stormed out of New York, Congress called the First Federal Congress to assemble on March 4, 1789. So bitter had been the debate that the ordinance avoided naming New York City as the place of meeting, by referring instead to the "present seat of Congress." The choice, Congressman Madison informed Washington, was either staying in New York or strangling the new government at its birth.[4]

A new day had dawned for the city of New York. Its narrow escape strengthened the resolve of New Yorkers to make their city even more pleasant for Congress and its members and thereby thwart all attempts to move the seat of government to Philadelphia. The lively social and political atmosphere of New York between 1785 and 1788 paled by comparison to what it became in 1789 and 1790. Immediately after Congress decided to remain in New York, its citizens began to talk about a better building for Congress to meet in, a palatial home for the president, and the creation of a "Republican Court" with audiences, levees, and established forms of etiquette. Most significantly, they began to refer to New York City as the federal capital. Not even the proud Philadelphians had thought of their city as the federal capital, for prior to the adoption of the Constitution the term "capital" had only been applied to seats of state government.[5]

New Yorkers had reason for pride in what they accomplished during the next six months. New docks jutted into the Hudson and East rivers, streets were repaved, a new steeple rose on Trinity Church, increased efforts were made to eliminate evidence of the great fires of a decade earlier, and newspapers debated the importance of better street lighting and a larger police force for the "seat of the American empire." The most important project undertaken by the New Yorkers was the conversion of City Hall at Wall and Nassau streets into an elegant building for the First Federal Congress. Pierre L'Enfant supervised the enlargement and redecoration of the eighty-five-year-old structure, which had housed the trial of John Peter Zenger and the Stamp Act Congress as well as the Confederation Congress. The speed with which the reconstruction took place stunned observers, and Federal Hall, the building's new name, quickly became a symbol for the new government throughout the United States. Although referred to as the "Hall" rather than as the "Capitol," the building served the same purpose. By 1790, the building also served as something of a museum, where visitors could see patent models and paintings, including some by John Trumbull.

On the night of March 3, 1789, New York City began a two-month long celebration of the birth of the new government with a thirteen-gun salute to the Union under the Articles of Confederation. The next morning an eleven-gun salute—not thirteen, because North Carolina and Rhode Island had not yet ratified—heralded the new Union. Church bells rang. On Federal Hall and other buildings flags snapped in the wind. New York had spared no pains to provide for the reception of Congress, or to make its stay agreeable, concluded Senator Oliver Ellsworth of Connecticut.

Inside the hall, members of the First Federal Congress gathered. No quorum formed in either the House or Senate. Their numbers slowly increasing day by day, the mortified members waited a month before getting down to formal business. They occupied themselves with political discussion, particularly over how to respond to the expected motion from the Pennsylvanians that Congress move to Philadelphia. Stressing the elegance of Federal Hall, the waste of time and money and the inconvenience of a move, New York "belles, beaux and clergymen" went door to door among congressmen urging them to oppose removal to Philadelphia. Madison and the southerners agreed with New York's partisans and refused to support the effort because it promised to immerse Congress in a morass of political wheeling and dealing which would delay implementation of the Constitution.[6]

Not all the visiting was political. Formal visits dominated: members of Congress visited each other, members visited prominent New Yorkers such as the Jays, Livingstons, Duers, and Temples, and soon after his arrival George Washington visited every member of Congress. Representative Daniel Hiester, Jr., of Pennsylvania had to replenish his supply of visiting cards. Senator William Paterson of New Jersey explained to his wife that visits had to be returned. Everyone, he claimed, was sick of it. Yet everyone did it because of the prevalence of fashion and the force of custom.[7]

Members also occupied themselves in March and April by becoming familiar with New York City. In 1789 it spanned only the tip of Manhattan Island, reaching as far north along the East River as the present-day Williamsburg Bridge. Despite the recent improvements, congressmen were not favorably impressed with the physical city and its polluted air. John Page observed that it could not be compared with Philadelphia in beauty and elegance. He complained particularly of the dirty, narrow, curved, and muddy streets where garbage-eating hogs ran free and the omnipresent water carts obstructed traffic. He characterized the architecture as an uninspiring hodgepodge of wooden, stone, and brick structures. A year later Fisher Ames of Massachusetts simply referred to the city as a pigsty perfumed by its wharves and gutters.[8]

Congressmen were less critical of their personal accommodations, other than the cost. Senator Rufus King and Rep. John Laurance, both of New York, had homes in the city as did Columbia College President William Samuel Johnson, a senator from Connecticut. Others like William Few of North Carolina and Elbridge Gerry of Massachusetts had wives from New York. Three Pennsylvania Representatives—the Muhlenberg brothers, Peter and Frederick, and Henry Wynkoop—moved into the homes of relatives. Senator William Maclay, also of Pennsylvania, lived first in the home of Wynkoop's cousin William Vandalsem. There, where the World Trade Center now towers, Maclay composed the majority of the diary which tells us so much about the First Congress and late eighteenth-century New York City. During the second session, Maclay resided with the Muhlenbergs at the home of their brother-in-law, Rev. John Kunze, pastor of the Lutheran Church on the northern edge of town, close to present-day City Hall. Vice President John Adams resided at Richmond Hill, an elevated country seat, halfway to Greenwich Village. Senator Richard Henry Lee of Virginia, who lived in the city when he served as president of Congress in 1785, chose in 1789 to go all the way to Greenwich Village. Those few members who brought their families tended to rent houses during the second session so as not to curtail their ability to entertain. During the first session, several congressional families had chosen the most common lodging arrangement, the boarding house.

Congressmen often picked a boarding house on the basis of what they had heard from men who had served in the Confederation Congress in New York. Lacking that recommendation, some stayed in the more expensive taverns for a few days until they found a suitable boarding house. Congressmen paid a fixed charge for room and board and additional amounts for dinner guests, firewood, and alcohol. Also available at additional cost was the assistance of servants who worked at the boarding house. Some members brought their own servants or rented such services from colleagues. When Daniel Hiester left Dorothy and Vandine Elsworth's Boarding House at 19 Maiden Lane, which was popular with the Pennsylvania and Virginia delegations, he took special care to tip the servants. Once having established a relationship with a particular boarding house and those who resided there, congressmen tended to return. Nevertheless, Thomas Fitzsimons made it clear that he and fellow Pennsylvanian George Clymer would not return to the same boarding house for the second session unless the owner employed a different cook because the food during the first session had been too bad to describe.

Additional services were generally not available at boarding houses. Congressmen sent their laundry to washerwomen. Barbering was regularly contracted out. Bathing also took place elsewhere. Bathhouses served the need in the winter, but public bathing was preferred in the summer. Then presidential aides, members of Congress, and other notables could be found bathing together in the Hudson River, although probably not in the company of the uninhibited New York boys, whose nude swims—even from the Battery—had not yet been outlawed.

Despite the demands created by members of Congress, boarding house keepers usually had room for out-of-towners. Some, like Robert Harris, came for surgery; others, like Isabella Bell and Samuel Davis, came as tourists to see the capital; still others came on commercial errands. Many had business to transact with the federal government: petitioners like the Revolutionary War doctor John Ely, and the inventor Leonard Harbaugh, who entertained New Yorkers with his models; jobseekers like Michael Morgan O'Brien and Sharp Delany; lobbyists like Manasseh Cutler of the Ohio Company and Pennsylvanian William Hamilton, who came to lobby for Lancaster as the permanent seat of the federal government; and federal officials like Arthur St. Clair, governor of the Northwest Territory, who arrived for consultation and seemed disinclined to return to his rustic post. Indeed, the lodging business was so good that a lady who had boarded state legislators at Boston moved to New York to open a boarding house for the Massachusetts delegation.[9]

By May 1789, most congressmen had settled into New York and a routine of daily activities. A typical weekday began about seven. After dressing, eating, and perhaps a horse ride for exercise, a member would walk to Federal Hall to attend a 9:00 A.M. committee meeting. Enroute he might mail letters at the post office, speak with an acquaintance, purchase lottery tickets, or give money to a needy person in the street. A few members preferred to be driven to Federal Hall, a practice that caused problems when Congress adjourned early and members had to wait for their carriages or coaches. If a member had no committee to attend, he might remain in his room working, reading the newspapers and congressional documents, or catching up on correspondence. Sometimes members used the opportunity to pen anonymous newspaper articles in support of or in opposition to measures pending before Congress.

Congress generally met from eleven in the morning until three or four in the afternoon, though members did not necessarily remain on the floor, especially during periods of routine business when quorum requirements were ignored. A congressman might choose to meet with visitors in the second-floor lobby, provide a constituent with a tour of Federal Hall, or huddle with colleagues in an attempt to resolve some issue politically. Not all who remained listened to the debates. Diversions included newspaper reading, conversations with colleagues, catching up on a usually voluminous correspondence, exchanging jokes about the vice president, or revising a House speech prior to its publication. Members paid close attention to the House debates as they appeared in the press. Both the *New York Daily Gazette* and the *Daily Advertiser* carried speeches made on the floor. In 1789, two entrepreneurs came to New York City to report the debates and founded publications that remain important historical sources. John Fenno established the *Gazette of the United States*, and Thomas Lloyd founded the *Congressional Register*, an occasional periodical which appeared sometimes weeks after the statements it printed were delivered. Fenno gave members the privilege of submitting to him revised versions of their speeches.

Noise was already a form of urban pollution, and Congress generated a certain quantity of its own. Street noises had to be ignored except when they reached intolerable levels, as they did when the June 1789 Freemason Parade passed by Federal Hall. A speech by Georgia Representative James Jackson, always delivered in a flamboyant style, could cause the Senate to shut its windows, even in July. The most persistent source of noise, however, was the House galleries. Attendance at debates was a popular pastime among New Yorkers of leisure, and quickly became an activity of New York high society, particularly among women. For visitors to New York, attendance was a ritual, as the diaries of Samuel Davis and young John Quincy Adams attest. The galleries were often filled to capacity. Observers remained for hours, cracking nuts and chattering with friends. Sometimes members contributed to the disruption by, in effect, speaking to the gallery, a practice which peaked when the Quakers attended to monitor debate on their anti-slavery petitions.[10]

Between daily adjournment and dinner a variety of matters kept congressmen occupied. Before leaving Federal Hall, a member might go upstairs to the New York Society Library to borrow a book. A short walk to the bookseller allowed members to purchase such volumes as Adam Smith's *Wealth of Nations*, Jedidiah Morse's *American Geography*, and Thomas Jefferson's *Notes on the State of Virginia*. A stop at the bookbinders to arrange for binding the individually published sections of the Congressional Record was routine, as was a visit to the stationers to purchase blank books or writing paper. Merchant members like Robert Morris of Pennsylvania and Jeremiah Wadsworth of Connecticut had businesses to oversee. One member arrived at New York with a shipload of tobacco to sell. For relaxation, congressmen might play nine pins, or visit one of the city's pleasure gardens, modeled after those in London. Flourishing especially in summer, these resorts specialized in tea, exotic plants—including citrus trees—and a variety of entertainments.

Congressmen could also employ the time to work. A member might meet with presidential aides David Humphreys or Tobias Lear to discuss an appointment for a constituent; or he might visit one of the executive departments to obtain information about a bill in committee or a petition from a constituent. Besides the flood of petitions and job applications, constituents made a great variety of requests. One woman asked her congressman to ask a local minister about a bequest she had not received and to ask the Georgia members if they knew anything about a brother from whom she had not heard in years.

The time before dinner might be spent sitting for a portrait. As the capital city, New York attracted artists who came to paint the portraits of the famous men of the Revolutionary generation gathered there. Benjamin Goodhue and Speaker of the House Frederick Muhlenberg sat for Joseph Wright. John Ramage painted miniatures of Elbridge Gerry and of Senator William Few and Catherine Few. George Washington and his family sat for Edward Savage. Historical paintings kept some artists occupied. John Trumbull sketched likenesses for his series on the great events of the American Revolution. William Dunlap exhibited at his studio an eight-by-twelve-foot *Inauguration of the President.* His *Youth Rescued from a Shark* also attracted attention.

Walks drew members into the life of the city. A long stroll into the countryside north of town provided enlightenment as well as exercise if one stopped at the Minto Estate to observe its agricultural improvements. Some particularly large cattle at the butchershop or the aftermath of the brewery fire on Catherine Street might be worth a visit. Some went down to the Fort George demolition site to see the exposed coffins of several New York royal governors, including Richard Coote who, the press reported, had an affinity for dressing in women's clothes. The fort was demolished to make way for the handsome presidential mansion which New York State decided to construct in 1790 as a means of encouraging Congress to remain in the city.[11]

Members usually ate dinner at their boarding houses. Sometimes a state delegation or other group would meet over dinner at a tavern to discuss political strategy. Those who found reading and writing by candlelight too taxing on their eyes could always find company and conversation in the boarding house, at a nearby tavern, or at a dinner which went into the evening. At times like these conversation might well focus on such local events as the ordeal of a bowery resident who was threatened with death and the burning of his house if he did not pay his assailant fifty guineas. More upsetting was the suicide of a man from Georgia, perhaps a Columbia College student. Northern congressmen were especially impressed by the reaction of the man's young slave, who had to be pulled from the body and prevented from killing himself. Duels always drew attention, especially if they involved members of Congress. In September 1789, Aaron Burr asked South Carolina Representative Aedanus Burke to be his second. And in April 1790 there was much excitement when Burke nearly engaged in a duel with Alexander Hamilton.[12]

After dinner, congressmen might read, write, or on rare occasions attend a six o'clock committee meeting. As the evening wore on, the absence of female companionship became difficult for some. Congressman Elias Boudinot of New Jersey wished that his wife could repay him with tenderness at the close of the day. Although Sarah Wynkoop and other congressional wives came to New York to visit their husbands and view the city's attractions, most members either remained alone or met New York women. A year before he married New Yorker Margaret Lowther, John Page, who one acquaintance described as a lecher, "was never less disposed to marry than now. Business & Dissipation & a great Variety of fine Figures divert the Attention from fixing on one Object. . . . I have seen no one yet who would suit me. The rich Widows are ugly & old & the rich maids too young." Joshua Seney of Maryland, John Vining of Delaware, and Issac Coles of Virginia also had married into New York families or did so during the First Congress. Senator Paine Wingate of New Hampshire in particular complained about a lack of female companionship, but he was careful not to repeat his earlier indiscretion, when, as a member of the Confederation Congress, he had an affair with his landlady. She demanded a sum of money which he refused to pay. Eventually, arbitrators negotiated a fair sum. Aedanus Burke's affair with his landlady during the First Congress ended in her pregnancy, and he supported the child for the rest of his life. Senator Maclay implied that Pennsylvanian Thomas Scott also fathered a child and claimed that Scott frequently spent the night away from his lodgings. Some Congressmen, as well as visitors attracted to the city because of its role as the capital, probably relied on New York's readily available prostitutes.[13]

Congress usually adjourned for the weekend. Members found it a good time to correspond with families and constituents. Some attended services at one of a variety of churches in the city. Though most could not return to their distant homes, they could hire horses or carriages to leave the capital on a variety of excursions. These trips took the form of short horseback or carriage rides on the roads which passed through the fields just north of the city or through the scenic upper part of Manhattan Island to Kingsbridge. Particularly popular was a fourteen-mile circuit of Manhattan. Longer trips might be made to Flatbush and Jamaica on Long Island. In the other direction, a ferry ride to New Jersey led members to Elizabethtown, New Brunswick, or Passaic to see the falls. Occasionally, parties went on fishing trips to Sandy Hook. In July 1789, several members sailed up the Hudson to West Point. Congress had been considering purchasing the site for years, but no one claimed that the junket was official.[14]

As early as June 1789 a visitor from Baltimore proclaimed that "The American Court. . . is as gay as any Court in Christendom." As important as Congress was to the creation of the "Republican Court," the presidency proved more so. This new institution, unlike Congress, lacked social precedents, and New Yorkers, like other Americans, saw similarities between the president and the king. Just as they took special pains to welcome Congress and involve its members in the life of the city, New Yorkers provided for the president. But in a society which believed in legislative supremacy, they followed the lead of Congress, or at least appeared to do so.

In April 1789, Congress appointed Samuel Osgood to provide,

at its expense, accommodations for the president. In a matter of days, thanks to weeks of unofficial, behind-the-scenes activity, Osgood's wife, Maria, and her friend Lady Kitty Duer, two of New York City's most cultured ladies, converted the Osgood residence, previously occupied by the presidents of the Confederation Congress, into an elegantly appointed presidential mansion. It was wallpapered on two floors, carpeted with the best Turkish rugs, and filled with fine furniture, china, and silver. The mansion faced onto Franklin Square, near the northeastern edge of town. It proved too small and in 1790 George Washington moved to the newly built Macomb Mansion on Broad Way. This placed the president at the center of the capital, near Federal Hall and the residences of the diplomatic corps.[15]

New Yorkers were also active in matters of social form relating to the presidency. While the Senate debated the question of establishing a title for the president, and Alexander Hamilton and others used "Your Excellency," the ladies of New York entitled the president, "His Highness." And when President Washington arrived in the city in April 1789, New Yorkers quickly switched the spotlight from Congress to the president. On April 24, Congress sent an official delegation to New Jersey to escort Washington to New York. Thirteen New York harbor pilots in white uniform manned an ornate barge, hung with red curtains, which carried Washington across the bay. Dozens of tall ships and small boats displayed their colors and naval ornaments. The *Galviston*, a Spanish warship, hoisted into its rigging the flags of two dozen nations and sounded a thirteen-gun salute as the crew manned its yards. Another thirteen-gun salute announced Washington's arrival at the red-carpeted stairs of Murray's Wharf, where an adoring crowd of several thousand lined the shore for half a mile from the Battery to the Paulus Hook ferry landing. Military units paraded. A band played the familiar patriotic tune, "God Save the King," which must have raised questions in the minds of some spectators, especially in the absence of its Americanized lyrics. More than any other single occurrence, this event, with its trappings of monarchy, set the tone for the Republican Court.

At night, many homes were elaborately illuminated with candle arrangements, and New Yorkers filled the streets in celebration. Governor George Clinton, also a resident of the city, welcomed Washington in a ceremony and at a dinner that evening which publicly acknowledged that the executive head of the federal government took precedence over the executive head of a state government.

Someone who disapproved of this adulation satirized the occasion in a cartoon entitled "The Entry," hawked on the streets of the capital. In it, Washington rode a jackass, led by his aide David Humphreys chanting hosannas and laying palm branches before him. A couplet stated:

> The glorious time has come to pass
> When David shall conduct an Ass.[16]

New Yorkers had far less to do with Washington's inauguration on April 30 than with his arrival because Congress exercised greater control on this occasion. The ceremony was, in any case, reserved. Its most exciting moment came when New York Chancellor Robert R. Livingston stepped forward to declare to the crowd, "Long Live George Washington, President of the United States." New Yorkers did celebrate in the evening. The French and Spanish ministers illuminated their homes and grand fireworks lit the sky. Young John Randolph of Roanoke, a student at Columbia, later described the event as a virtual coronation. The ceremony, of course, drew many visitors to the capital, among them Thomas Jefferson's nephew Peter Carr, who James Madison had brought with him to witness the birth of the new nation.[17]

Conscious of setting precedent and of the raging public debate over the monarchial potential of the new government, Washington inquired of Alexander Hamilton, James Madison, John Adams, and John Jay about the proper line of social conduct for him to follow with Congress and the public. Two of these men were New Yorkers and very much part of the city's gentle society. Hamilton modeled his reply after European custom, attempting to exalt the institution of the presidency as high as possible: "Men's minds are prepared for a pretty high tone in the demeanour of the Executive; but I doubt whether for so high a tone as in the abstract might be desireable."[18]

After reviewing the responses, Washington instituted the levee, a social event similar to a formal reception. At first he held them on Tuesday and Friday afternoons just after Congress

Located at the foot of Broadway, the building with the classical portico was intended to be the residence of President Washington, but he never occupied it. It became the residence of Governors George Clinton and John Jay, was then used for the custom house, and was torn down in 1815. It is presented as it appeared in 1797, as published in Stokes, The Iconography of Manhattan Island.

adjourned for the day. Soon the Friday levee became an evening "assembly" with Martha Washington "at home" as hostess. Others followed suit and by the second session there was an "at home" every evening of the week. Abigail Adams held hers on Monday at the vice presidential mansion. On Tuesday Lady Elizabeth Temple, wife of British consul Sir John Temple, entertained. Lucy Knox, wife of Secretary of War Henry Knox, always provided at least one game of whist at her Wednesday affairs. On Thursdays, Sarah Jay, wife of Chief Justice John Jay, opened her home. To these assemblies came congressmen, federal officials, people of social rank in New York, and distinguished visitors to the capital.

These assemblies, and the less formal private parties, provided opportunities for political discussion among New Yorkers and federal officials. On the day that Secretary of the Treasury Alexander Hamilton made his Report on Public Credit, Assistant Secretary of the Treasury William Duer impressed guests at Walter Rutherfurd's party with his financial knowledge. One of the most active stock and land speculators in the United States, Duer was the first federal official to resign because of a scandal. Its details are unknown, but probably involved insider trading.[19]

In addition to the levees, assemblies, and parties, balls occurred at least once a month. May 1789 was an especially active month with a federal ball on May 7 and the elegant French minister's ball a week later, both in honor of the newly inaugurated president. Dinner parties occurred routinely. Following one Tuesday levee in February 1790, Senator William Paterson had four or five invitations for dinner, including perhaps the one held by the French consul to celebrate the Franco-American alliance. The most important dinners, of course, were those at the presidential mansion. These multi-course affairs, hosted by President and Mrs. Washington, included more than a dozen guests and at least one presidential aide. These affairs were formal and rather stiff, but no one declined to attend, not even shy Senator Maclay. If Chief Justice John Jay was present, the men could expect an off-color story after the ladies withdrew. In February 1790 everyone celebrated the birthday of George Washington. The annual celebration of the king's birthday had already been transferred to Washington, although some New Yorkers continued to celebrate the birthday of King George III as well.[20]

A variety of activities in the city, in particular the theater, enhanced the Republican Court. Philadelphia had outlawed the theater until 1789, when it legalized the art as part of an effort to attract Congress away from New York, and by the late eighteenth century American theater was virtually synonymous with New York City. Revived in 1785 when Congress moved to town, the Old American Company provided Shakespeare, Addison and Steele, and Sheridan as well as American playwrights at the John Street Theater. The 1789 season ran from April 14 to December 15 and included comedies, tragedies, farces, and pantomimes. President and Mrs. Washington had their own box, and when he was in attendance performances opened with the "President's March," later known as "Hail Columbia."

Concerts included dancing and refreshments and were exclusive affairs governed by strict rules of conduct. The musical program might include Bach and Haydn as well as lesser-known figures. Alexander Reinagle was the reigning conductor and composer. He had returned to New York from Philadelphia at the end of 1788 as one of several Americans who looked to the federal capital as the cultural center of the United States. Private tutors offered instruction in music and dance, and Alexander White of Virginia employed them for his daughters whom he brought to the capital during the second session of the First Congress.[21]

New York attracted a variety of entertainers and showmen. So much so that Rep. Sedgwick complained about fellow members who prolonged congressional sessions because New York provided so many amusements. Bowen's Waxworks had likenesses of both George Washington and George III. Exotic animals—such as a pair of orangutans, a baboon, a sloth, an anteater, and a tiger—visited the city in 1789. Showman Joseph Decker proved the hit of that season. His first enterprise was as a ventriloquist with a dummy which answered questions. Gadgets including burglar and fire alarm systems also composed his repertoire. Best known for his hot air balloons, the first to be seen in North America, Decker's July and August ascensions came down in the East River. The September 1789 event, which caused an adjournment of Congress, attracted two-thirds of the residents to the flats north of the city, and ended when the balloon caught fire.

Special events added to the social life of the city. Among the first after the inauguration was the special cavalry assembly in honor of the arrival of Martha Washington at the end of May 1789. Fourth of July celebrations in 1789 and 1790 included military parades, orations, and a party at the president's. March 1790 saw the rededication of Trinity Church with its ornate presidential box. In May 1790 members of the Tammany Society, dressed as Indians, paraded through the streets of New York in a grotesque contrast to perhaps the grandest of all the special events. In July 1790 New York hosted the first head of a foreign state to visit the United States capital when Alexander McGillivray, half-breed king of the Creek Indian Nation, arrived with an entourage of thirty warriors. He first visited Washington at the presidential mansion and then Governor Clinton. Locking arms with Secretary of War Henry Knox and presidential aide David Humphreys, McGillivray paraded through the streets of the city to the Battery where at a special ceremony they smoked a peace pipe.[22]

Congressmen and those attached to the federal government praised the hospitality of New Yorkers in 1790 as much as they had in 1785. Even Maclay, who filled his diary with complaints about New York City, concluded on his last day at the capital that its allurements were more than five to one compared with Philadelphia, which he considered the most unsocial of cities. New Yorkers of course had reason to be hospitable: federal officeholders poured money into the local economy, business flourished as did culture and amusements, and population rose. New Yorkers took a keen interest in federal politics. They followed the congressional investigation of Robert Morris's accounts from his tenure as superintendent of finance for the Confederation Congress. According to Maclay, they also lobbied against higher duties on British trading vessels and in favor of higher federal salaries. When the House debated Secretary of the Treasury Hamilton's *Report on Public Credit* "nothing else was heard of, even among the women and children"[23]

All this ended when the sword of Damocles fell in July 1790. Congress's decision to move to Philadelphia until a federal city could be built on the Potomac River enraged New Yorkers, who lost not only the federal government but also those dependent on it. Publishers Thomas Lloyd and John Fenno went to Philadelphia to publish the debates of Congress. So too did dozens of tradesmen. Stinging cartoons attacking George Washington and members of Congress circulated in the streets while critical newspaper articles filled the press. One called for federal aid in the wake of the disaster. Others criticized Congress for its ingratitude or condemned the New York ratifying convention for falling for the promise that the city would remain the capital. Some New Yorkers found personal attacks on congressmen cathartic. The Pennsylvania delegation in particular felt the barbs during their last uncomfortable month at New York when the rabble took to yelling the cartoon captions at them.

A final though uncommon theme in the New York press was "so what, who cared?" The civic improvements occasioned by the residence of Congress might not have been made for half a century. Would parties and the drama cease? On the contrary! Would no more streets be paved? One writer predicted that, with the opening of a canal along the Mohawk River, New York City would become the great emporium of the new world, concluding that the advantages of being the capital of the United States paled in comparison to such an endless source of wealth, grandeur, and influence.[24]

Notes

1. For additional discussion of New York City in 1789 and 1790 see Thomas E. V. Smith, *The City of New York In The Year of Washington's Inauguration, 1789* (New York, 1889); Frank Monaghan and Marvin Lowenthal, *This Was New York, The Nation's Capital in 1789* (Garden City, N.Y. 1943); Sidney I. Pomerantz, *New York, An American City, 1783–1803, A Study of Urban Life* (Port Washington, N.Y., 1938); Rufus W. Griswold, *The Republican Court; or American Society in the Days of Washington* (New York, 1868); and I. N. Phelps Stokes, *The Iconography of Manhattan Island, 1498–1909,* 6 vols. (New York, 1967).

2. Kenneth R. Bowling, *The Creation of Washington, D.C., The Idea and Location of the American Capital* (Fairfax, Virginia, 1990), chap. 1.

3. Ibid., chap. 2.

4. Ibid., chap. 3; Pomerantz, *New York,* 102–104.

5. Baron Von Steuben to William North, September 18, 1788, *American Art Galleries Catalog* (n.p.: American Art Association, Inc., 1929), item 140; George Clymer to Benjamin Rush. [June 1789], *The American Scene, A Panorama of Autographs* (Boston, 1983), item 80.

6. Bowling, *Creation,* chap. 3; Charlene Bangs Bickford and Kenneth R. Bowling, *Birth of the Nation: The First Federal Congress, 1789–1791* (Madison, Winsconsin, 1989), 9–12; (Philadelphia) *Independent Gazetteer,* January 5, March 9, 1789; Oliver Ellsworth to Abigail Ellsworth, March 9, 1789, Oliver Ellsworth Papers, Connecticut Historical Society.

7. Daniel Hiester, Memorandums, 1789, Historical Society of Berks County (hereinafter cited as Hiester); Alexander White to Adam Stephen, March 24, 1789, Adam Stephen Papers, Library of Congress; Elizabeth Burr to Betsy Sher-

man, April 19, 1789, Baldwin Family Papers, Yale University; Samuel Johnston to James Iredell, January 30, 1790, Griffith J. McRee, *The Life and Correspondence of James Iredell*, 2 vols. (New York, 1949), 2:279; William Paterson to Euphemia Paterson, March 27, 1789, William Paterson Papers, Rutgers University.

8. John Page to Robert Page, March 16, 1789, *Virginia Magazine of History and Biography* 43 (1935), 290; Elias Boudinot to Hannah Boudinot, May 15, 1789, Boudinot Papers, Rutgers University; Fisher Ames to Thomas Dwight, June 27, 1790, Fisher Ames Papers, Dedham Historical Society; Theodore Sedgwick to Pamela Sedgwick, June 14, 1790, Sedgwick Family Papers, Massachusetts Historical Society.

9. *The New York Directory, and Register for the Year 1789* (New York, 1789), 101–102; Abigail Adams to Mary Cranch, August 9, 1789, Abigail Adams Papers, American Antiquarian Society; Thomas Fitzsimons to Samuel Meredith, December 7, 1789, Dreer Collection, Historical Society of Pennsylvania; Hiester; Roger Sherman to Rebecca Sherman, February 1790, *The Collector* 58 (1945–46), item 2648; Henry Wynkoop to Reading Beattie, March 9, 1789, *Pennsylvania Magazine of History and Biography* 38 (1914), 46; William Hamilton to Benjamin H. Smith, August 30, 1789, ibid., 39 (1915), 156; *New York Daily Gazette*, May 7, 22, July 17, 1789; Theodore Sedgwick to Pamela Sedgwick, August 1, 20, 1789, Sedgwick Family Papers, Massachusetts Historical Society; John Stevens, Jr., to John Stevens, Sr., July 9, 1789, Stevens Family Papers, New Jersey Historical Society; Robert Lewis, Diary, August 2, 1789, Mount Vernon Ladies Association of the Union; Pomerantz, *New York*, 499–500; Samuel Meredith to Margaret Meredith, July 7, 1790, Samuel Meredith Letters, Library Company of Philadelphia Collections at the Historical Society of Pennsylvania; Kenneth R. Bowling and Helen E. Veit, *The Diary of William Maclay and Other Notes on Senate Debates* (Baltimore, 1988) (hereinafter *Maclay*), 6–7, 153, 178, 260–61, 284, 325.

10. *Maclay*, 88, 150, 226, 262, 274; Hiester; Elias Boudinot to Hannah Boudinot, April 14, 1789, Boudinot Papers, Princeton University; John Quincy Adams, Diary, September 17–18, 21–26, 1789, Adams Family Manuscript Trust, Massachusetts Historical Society; John Page to St. George Tucker, June 6, 1790, Tucker-Coleman Papers, College of William and Mary; Theodore Sedgwick to Pamela Sedgwick, February 9, March 4, 1790, Sedgwick Papers, Massachusetts Historical Society; Abraham Baldwin to Ruth Barlow, July 3, 1789, Henry E. Huntington Library; Fisher Ames to Thomas Dwight, July 25, 1790, Fisher Ames Papers, Dedham Historical Society; Samuel Davis, Journal, September 17, 18, 1789. Massachusetts Historical Society; Manasseh Cutler, Journal, February 22—April 9, 1790, Northwestern University; George Washington to David Stuart, July 26, 1789, George Washington Papers, Library of Congress; Bickford and Bowling, *Birth of the Nation*, 28; John Pemberton to James Pemberton, February 11, 1790, Pennsylvania Abolition Society Papers, Historical Society of Pennsylvania; (New York) *Daily Advertiser*, June 10, 1790; *New York Daily Gazette*, June 26, 1790.

11. Samuel Davis, Journal, September 16, 18, 1789, Massachusetts Historical Society; *Maclay*, 20, 51, 75, 218, 252, 297; Hiester; Smith, *New York*, 116; Pomerantz, *New York*, 468; Donald Hackson and Dorothy Twohig, eds., *The Diaries of George Washington*, 6 vols. (Charlottesville, Virginia, 1976–79), 5:451, 478, 490, 509; 6: 36–40, 57; *New York Daily Gazette*, June 18, 1790; Margaret C. S. Christman, *The First Federal Congress, 1789–1791* (Washington, D.C., 1989), p. 267; Walter Rutherfurd to John Rutherfurd, February 13, 1790, Rutherfurd

Papers, New-York Historical Society; William Hartshorne to Robert Bowne, Blount Papers, North Carolina Department of Archives and History.

12. William Paterson to Euphemia Paterson, February 6, 1790, William Paterson Papers, Rutgers University; Paine Wingate to Mary Wiggin, February 27, 1790, Wingate Papers, Harvard University; Peter Silvester to [Peter Van Schaack?], May 26, 1789, Miscellaneous Manuscripts, New-York Historical Society; Theodore Sedgwick to Pamela Sedgwick, June 19, 1789, Sedgwick Papers, Massachusetts Historical Society; *Maclay*, 235, 298.

13. John Page to St. George Tucker, May 3, 1789, Tucker-Coleman Papers, College of William and Mary; William North to Benjamin Walker, May 9, 1790, Lloyd W. Smith Collection, Morristown National Historic Park; Elias Boudinot to Hannah Boudinot, April 14, 1789, Boudinot Papers, Princeton University; *Maclay*, 206, 209, 218, 298; William Plumer, "Paine Wingate," *New Hampshire State Papers* 21(1892), 829–30; John Meleney, *The Public Life of Aedanus Burke: Revolutionary Republican* (Columbia, South Carolina, 1989), 30–31; Monaghan and Lowenthal, *New York*, 219; Christman, *First Congress*, 233.

14. Hiester; *Maclay*, 70, 252; Theodore Sedgwick to Pamela Sedgwick, June 14, 1790, Sedgwick Papers, Massachusetts Historical Society; William Smith to Otho Holland Williams, July 22, 1789, Otho Holland Williams Papers, Maryland Historical Society; Pomerantz, *New York*, 498.

15. Otho Holland Williams to Phillip Thomas, June 7, 1789, Otho Holland Williams Papers, Maryland Historical Society.

16. Dorothy Twohig, ed., *The Papers of George Washington, Presidential Series* (Charlottesville, Virginia, 1987), 2:156–57; Fisher Ames to William Tudor, April 25, 1789, Massachusetts Historical Society *Collections* 8(1826), 317–18; M. Otis to Hannah Smith, May 1, 1789, Norcross Papers, Massachusetts Historical Society; John Armstrong to Horatio Gates, April 7, 1789, Gates Papers, New York Public Library; Henry Sewall, Diary, April 26, 1789, Massachusetts Historical Society; Smith, *New York*, 222; (New York) *Gazette of the United States*, April 22–25, 1789.

17. *Maclay*, 27–40; Samuel B. Webb to Killian K. Van Rensselaer, March 22, 1789, Emmet Collection, New York Public Library; Douglass Adair, *Fame and the Founding Fathers* (New York, 1974), 190; John Randolph to Thomas Tucker, December 13, 1813, William C. Bruce, *John Randolph of Roanoke*, (New York, 1922), 74.

18. *Maclay*, 13; Twohig, *Washington, Presidential Series*, 2:211–14, 245–50, 312–14.

19. Abigail Adams to Mary Cranch, January 24, 1790. Abigail Adams Papers, American Antiquarian Society; Walter Rutherfurd to John Rutherfurd, January 9, 1790, Rutherfurd Papers, New-York Historical Society; Henry Sewall, Diary, May 7, 1790, Massachusetts Historical Society.

20. Alexander White to Horatio Gates, March 13, 1790. Emmet Collection, New York Public Library; William Paterson to Euphemia Paterson, February 6, 1790, Paterson Papers, Rutgers University; Henry Wynkoop to Reading Beattie, May 15, 1789, *Pennsylvania Magazine of History and Biography* 38 (1914), 54; Elias Boudinot to Hannah Boudinot, May 15, 1789, Boudinot Papers, Rutgers University; *New York Journal*, February 25, 1790; *Maclay*, 69, 137.

21. Alexander White to Horatio Gates, March 13, 1790, Emmet Collection, New York Public Library; Smith, *New York*, 171–79; Monaghan and Lowenthal, *New York*, 125.

22. Pomerantz, *New York*, 485–86; Henry Sewall, Diary, May 28, 1790, Massachusetts Historical Society; Hiester; Allyn Mather to Ebenezer Bernard,

July 22, 1790, Mather-Bernard Letters, Connecticut Historical Society; *Maclay*, 101, 265, 312; Jonas S. Addams to Richard Treat, September 25, 1789, Toner Collection, Library of Congress; Manasseh Cutler, Journal, March 25, 1790, Northwestern University; Smith, *New York*, 183–88.

23. Alexander White to Horatio Gates, March 13, 1790, Emmet Collection, New York Public Library; Martha Washington to Mercy Warren, June 12, 1790, Massachusetts Historical Society *Collections* 73(1925) 319; *Maclay*, 69, 74–75, 96, 143, 200, 310, 331; Mary Rogers to Mrs. Hudson, March 26, 1790, Letters of Anna Rodgers Hudson, New York Public Library; Frederick A. Muhlenberg to Benjamin Rush, January 9, 1790, Berol Collection, Columbia University; William Neilson to John Chaloner, February 17, 1790. Chaloner Papers, Clements Library, University of Michigan.

24. Bowling, *Creation*, chap. 7; William L. Smith to Edward Rutledge, November 24, 1790, William L. Smith Papers, South Carolina Historical Society.

James Duane, about 1784. Oil on canvas by Robert Edge Pine. Courtesy of the New-York Historical Society.

Federal New York: Mayors of the Nation's First Capital

Leo Hershkowitz

The brief period that was Federal New York is probably best remembered for the city's triumphant celebration of the ratification of the Constitution and the subsequent inauguration of President George Washington, who took the oath of office on April 30, 1789, on the balcony of Federal Hall. Formerly City Hall, the building, a gift from the city, was now the new nation's first capitol, just as the city itself had become the nation's center of government. These were proud days when, at least for a time, memories of British occupation, destruction, and turmoil were eased by pleasing prospects of a bright future. There was reason for optimism. New York had become the residence and place of business of the president and his cabinet, of members of Congress, of judges of the federal courts. The business of the nation and the state was conducted in gracious homes, inns and coffee houses, as well as in the halls of the capitol—all within the bounds of a burgeoning New York—and the streets of the small city were now marked by the coming and going of leaders from other parts of the country and representatives of the world's leading nations.

It was a heady scene, a time of pre-eminence, and James Duane and Richard Varick, the first mayors of the post-war city, were very much part of it. Like so many of their distinguished contemporaries, they were of a leadership drawn from propertied gentry, an aristocratic elite, that sought and held office as an obligation to perform public service. A desire for political power or some form of material gain must also have influenced these men, but if they sought the city's highest office to acquire lasting fame, they would be disappointed. While Duane and Varick were successful men, well known in their own day, they are known to present-day New Yorkers only as the names attached to two streets in lower Manhattan. But, questions of immortality aside, the careers of the first mayors were, like the early years of Federal New York, important to the making of a new urban society.

These were watershed years that saw the transformation of a colonial society into the beginnings of a system of democratic capitalism—years that marked the creation of the city's first banks and insurance companies and the birth of what would become the New York Stock Exchange. New York was on its way to becoming the principal financial center of the country. Trade expanded in new directions. The first American ships left New York on voyages to the Pacific and China. Others sailed to the Baltic and Mediterranean Seas. New York would soon be the nation's major port, to which came a growing number of newcomers. Thousands of immigrating New Englanders would have a major influence on the city's economic and social structure, while others from all parts of western Europe insured the diversity that had characterized the city from its beginnings.

The first steps toward enlarging the suffrage were taken during these years, and with it the emergence of modern political parties. Hospitals were built or expanded, a public school system was begun, and the foundation was laid for a modern water supply. Within a decade, the city would adopt its famed ''gridiron plan'' which was the foundation for the future city of skyscrapers. Clearly, the federal period of New York City's history, the years in which the city was administered by its first post-Revolutionary War mayors, were genuinely formative years that deserve serious historical consideration.

The Duane Years, 1784–1789

On November twenty-fifth, 1783, American troops led by General George Washington, Governor George Clinton, and General Henry Knox, made a ''triumphant entry'' into New York so ending almost 120 years of British rule, the last seven under military occupation. On the same day, known traditionally as "Evacuation Day," the last of the British units left the city. A week later, Washinton took leave of his officers at Fraunces Tavern and began a journey home and seemingly to retirement from public life. New York City and the rest of the nation were left to build a new society and to find answers to the tangled problems left by war and revolution.

The city that the British left behind was a tiny community when compared to the modern urban giant. In 1771, New York's population was 21,863 persons, most residing on Manhattan Island in an area below Wall Street, with some living on adjacent islands—Blackwell (now F.D. Roosevelt), Bucking (Ellis), Bedloe's or Kennedy (Liberty) and Nutten (Governor's). There were 3,137 blacks, most of whom were slaves. By the start of the Revolution a visitor estimated the city's population at between twenty-six and thirty thousand, with slaves composing at least a fifth of the total. These figures were indicative of unparalleled growth that had occurred between 1756 and 1776. In 1703 there were 4,375 New Yorkers and in 1756, 13,046.[1] The city witnessed equally significant economic development. For example, in 1756 exports to Great Britain totaled £24,023, in 1775 it stood at £187,108 while imports from Britain were £437,937 in 1774, up from £250425 in 1756, but, as a result of the political crisis, were only £1,118 in 1775. It was the only time that New York had held a favorable balance of trade since at least 1751.[2] New York was obviously a thriving, growing center. Though not quite the equal of Boston, Philadelphia, or Charleston in point of trade or population, it was rapidly overtaking these cities. This process of becoming first would be completed by the beginning of the nineteenth century.

The war had temporarily halted the city's expansion as population fluctuated wildly, with thousands of billeted troops and refugees swelling the number of inhabitants or, as they left, reducing it. When the British left in 1783, the city's population comprised an estimated 12,000 people forming a "heterogeneous set of inhabitants, composed of almost ruined exiles, disbanded soldiery, mixed foreigners, disaffected Tories, and the refuse of the British army."[3] Thousands left New York as Tory refugees. Having to choose between the wilderness of Canada or poverty in England or stay and face the anger of patriots, many chose Canada or England. These individuals, often the most noted and talented, included Judge William Smith, Jr., author of the first history of the province, who went to Canada and the untamed forest. General Oliver De Lancey and his fami- ly went to England, as did Judges John Tabor Kempe and Thomas Kempe. Gone, too, were the Robinsons, Philipses, and members of the Watts, Jauncey, and Low families. Merchants, lawyers, and doctors, as well as artisans, became exiles. New York lost a great many of its most accomplished citizens.[4]

There were other losses as well. In 1776 and in 1778, large sections of the city were swept by fire. The flames destroyed Trinity Church and most of the East River waterfront. The first fire, possibly intentionally set on orders from American officers in an attempt to hinder British occupation, was followed by a second in 1778 which created additional hardship, especially for civilians who were already coping with a serious housing shortage caused by the first fire, and living in make-shift hovels. One solution to the housing shortage was to create ''Canvass Town,'' a series of tents, located mainly along the East River, which provided ready shelter but created an early slum iden- tified with prostitution, poverty, and crime. The area was also known as ''Holy Ground.'' The war did not necessarily create all such problems, but it often made them worse. Physical con- ditions were appalling. Roads, streets, and wharves were in poor repair. Lamps had been destroyed. Civic buildings like the Bridewell or Alms House had been used as barracks or stables by the British military. Though the British had tried to establish in New York a model example of the benefits of British law and order as an object lesson for warring Americans, they could not control fire or unsettled economic conditions, nor could they do much about the weather which during the occupation was very severe. During the winter of 1779-1780, the Upper Bay and the Hudson River froze solid. Carriages were driven across the ice from Manhattan to Staten Island, and the British re-enforced their garrison because they feared that Washington would at- tack the island by using the frozen river as a convenient high- way.

With the end of occupation, civilian authority in the city was quickly restored. The state constitution of 1777 confirmed the well-known Montgomerie Charter of 1731—based on early charters including the Nicolls Charter of 1665 and the Dongan

Charter of 1686—which granted New York its corporate status. There were, however, some notable changes: A Council of Appointment, presided over by the governor and including one senator from each of the four senatorial districts into which the state was divided, now chose the mayor, city clerk, sheriff, recorder, and coroner. This had been solely the prerogative of the royal governor with advice and consent of his council. Little else changed. Aldermen and assistants, assessors, collectors, and constables were still elected each year by the city's qualified voters divided among its seven wards.

City elections were, until 1800, traditionally held on September 29. Suffrage was granted to any white male who was twenty-one years old and over, a freeholder, and a resident of the city for three months and of the ward for a month before election. A freeholder had to possess land or tenements in excess of twenty pounds or pay forty shillings in rent. This was reduced to twenty-five dollars in 1804. The coming of democracy, though slow, was apparent. Between 1790 and 1801 an estimated 5 to 10 percent of the population voted in city elections—some 3,000 in 1790 out of a population of 33,131 and some 2,900 in 1801. In the state elections of that year, some 13 percent of the state's 60,489 residents went to the polls.[5]

In city elections until 1804 each voter made his choice orally, though ballots were used in state elections from 1777 on.

The initial step in re-establishing city government came on December 10, 1783 when the Council for the Southern District— a body created in 1779 consisting of the governor and a large group of judges, senators and assemblymen, attorney general, chancellor, and secretary of state—handed over the reigns of authority to the electorate of the city by announcing that municipal elections would be held on December 15 for the selection of aldermen and assistant aldermen. In these early contests, bitter political animosity was evident and the old misalignment of Whigs versus Tory, Sons of Liberty versus "men of property," once more rattled through the streets. Radicals— John Lamb, Alexander McDougall, and Isaac Sears—were triumphant for the moment. Marinus Willett was chosen sheriff and Robert Benson, also with Sons of Liberty endorsements, became city clerk. The City Council itself was largely made up of merchants, lawyers, and a minority of tradesmen or "mechanics." Generally, however, despite the Sons of Liberty, the government of New York was basically in the hands of men of social and economic standing, those whose "vested interests" entitled them to office. This pattern varied but little from that of the colonial city.

James Duane was a case in point. In 1767, Duane refused a civic appointment in New York because it "led into party and dirty politicks. . .beneath a man who would wish to be honest and wise."[6] After the Revolution, however, Duane viewed political office from a different perspective. Radical victories needed to be balanced by the election of conservatives. On January 23, 1784, city fathers wrote to Governor George Clinton recommending the appointment of Duane as mayor, emphasizing the need for a lawyer to untangle the desperate state or municipal affairs. In 1784, Clinton and the Council of Appointment asked Duane to serve as mayor. He accepted the unsolicited office on February 5, 1784 and was formally installed on February 7, beginning a new life of public service. The induction ceremonies were held at the inn of John Simmons, on Wall Street at the head of Broad Street, not far from City Hall. The inn largely served the weekly meetings of the Common Council through the early months of 1784. With characteristic generosity, Duane informed his fellow councilmen that although it was customary to hold a public entertainment on such an occasion, the great distress and suffering prevalent in the City had a prior claim on his bounty. He donated twenty guineas to be used for "relief of my suffering fellow citizens—."[7]

Duane was an excellent choice; problems of the municipality called for just such an accomplished, experienced and influential man to direct the affairs of the city. In his almost six years as mayor, he proved to be a skillful administrator and an able leader in the work of municipal reconstruction. He was the first to hold the position following the Revolution and, therefore, became the city's first American mayor. His fellow townsmen seem to have regarded him as an appropriate choice on the basis of his contributions to the American cause.[8] And his career does indeed place him among the most influential and active New Yorkers in the great events of the Revolutionary War era.

One of five sons of Althea Ketteltas (1685–1736) and Anthony Duane (1682–1747), James was born in New York City on February 6, 1733. His parents were Dutch-Irish and members, if not mainstays, of the Anglican Church. His father had been an officer in the British Navy but resigned in favor of his mercantile business in New York. At an early age James decided to practice law, but rather than attend the Inns of Court in London, he spent seven years of study in the law office of James Alexander, a Scotsman and an able, if not inspiring, lawyer. Duane was admitted to practice in 1754 and soon enjoyed a lucrative and extensive law business. He was a "sound and conservative legalist," whose "briefs and agreements were thoroughly prepared and bristled with citations of British precedents and great writers."[9] Duane's career in public service began in his twenties. He was appointed clerk of the chancery court in 1762, attorney general in 1767, and boundary commissioner in 1768.

While Duane's rise was the result of his skill in law and politics, he also made an advantageous marriage. He allied himself with the influential Livingston family through marriage to Maria (Mary) Livingston (1739–1821)—oldest daughter of Colonel Robert Livingston—on October 21, 1759, at Livingston Manor. They were an attractive and socially active couple. While James met the obligations of his professional life, he and Mary were in frequent attendance at social affairs in New York City and also travelled occasionally to Philadelphia, to the eastern end of Long Island, and to Livingston Manor. The couple had ten children, but only five survived to adulthood.

Duane was caught up in the spirit of pre-Revolutionary politics and championed colonial rights. In 1764, he denounced an attempt on the part of Acting Governor Cadwallader Colden to review a jury decision in the case of *Forsey v. Cunningham.* The case established the principle in New York that no fact properly tried by a jury could be retried. Duane's objections were upheld by a British attorney general. In 1768, he defended James Jauncey, a conservative, against the radical John Morin Scott, leader of the "Republican" faction in New York, in a matter of a disputed election. Jauncey obtained his Assembly seat.

As the Revolution drew near, Duane had to make difficult political choices. Like Locke and Montesquieu, he firmly believed that liberty required obedience to law. "God forbid," he wrote in 1770, "that we should ever be so miserable as to sink to a Republick!"[10] He was a strong admirer of British constitutional government. But events did thrust themselves upon him and put his political philosophy to the test. New York City became a focal point for anti-British activity and at the same time was a center of comparatively conservative thought. The colony's leaders therefore faced the growing tension between colonies and mother country in a deliberate and organized manner. In May 1774, the people of New York City chose a Committee of Fifty-one "to correspond with the neighboring colonies on the impending crisis." Duane, described by John Adams as a man with a "sly surveying eye, a little squint-eyed—very sensible—and very artful," was a member of this committee, which was the first body in the colonies organized for definite action.[11] On May 23, it urged upon other colonies the assembling of an intercolonial congress. The Continental Congress probably owed its origin to this committee. On July 4, five men were selected to be submitted to the freeholders for approval at the polls. These five would represent New York at the First Continental Congress in Philadelphia. Philip Livingston, John Alsop, Isaac Sears, James Duane, and John Jay were chosen.

Like other New York conservatives, Duane wanted the newly convened Congress to follow a moderate, conciliatory policy toward England, one that involved a type of American home rule while recognizing British imperial authority. But radicals, led by John and Samuel Adams, Richard Henry Lee, and Patrick Henry, gained control over that Congress, and swayed their colleagues to a more revolutionary course. Though there was at first no drive toward independence by Congress, there was a strong effort to bring about a repeal of offensive English taxation. Duane and fellow New Yorker John Jay gained some concessions regarding Parliament's right to regulate external commerce, but they were less successful in gaining acknowledgement that ties between England and the colonies were based on common law and statutes. The radical element of Congress insisted on concepts of natural law and the inalienability of certain universal rights. However, all conciliatory maneuvers failed in the face of rapidly escalating events: The Boston and New York Tea Parties, Intolerable Acts, passing of the Suffolk Resolves, and the battles of Bunker Hill and Lexington and Concord. Conciliation became a casualty of rebellion and gunpowder.

While Duane was not a member of the New York delegation to the Second Continental Congress when it signed the Declaration of Independence, he obviously had joined the cause. Perhaps he felt that his large land holdings, including lands held in dispute in New Hampshire, would be jeopardized if he became a loyalist. Perhaps independence would enable free, able, hard-working men of property to save America from the ex-

cesses of democracy and so establish an aristocracy of intelli-
gence to balance the passions of the common people.[12] Duane
had a dream for a new more productive country. In 1775, he
wrote to his father-in-law Robert Livingston, "If we survive the
present storm, and Liberty should be secured for our Country,
it will become the favorite Residence of the Industrious from
all parts of the world, and a Rich Encrease of our Estates will
compensate our Losses. . . ."[13] Property and liberty made Duane
a rebel by necessity and a Federalist by persuasion.

During the war, Duane was a member of both the Continental Congress and the New York Provincial Congress. He helped
draft the Articles of Confederation and led a busy life raising
money and supplies and, in general, being particularly useful
to the American cause. The New York Provincial Congress was
the first revolutionary body to outline a new intercolonial program to finance the war. On May 30, 1775, the provincial congress instructed its delegates at the Second Continental Congress to propose that it was clearly impossible to raise by taxes
a sum adequate to the public service and that the Continental
government should issue paper money with a specific percentage of the total guaranteed by each colony. The Continental
Congress adopted the New York plan and put forward
$3,000,000 in paper. Duane chaired the responsible committee.[14]
New York and Duane deserve credit for having suggested the
monetary system that was used to finance the Revolution.

As the war progressed, Duane became one of the most influential members of Congress. He was a leader in Continental
relations with the Iroquois, and attended several Indian conferences. His belief that a "detachment of Continental Forces"
was necessary to subdue the Iroquois was influential in the decision to send a military expedition under General John Sullivan
into western New York.[15] The Iroquois remained a military
threat, but the expedition cut a destructive swath through their
western heartland and effectively ended their long-term influence in New York affairs.

Duane was also involved in matters relating to boundary
disputes, fund raising, and civil and military matters in general.
By 1781 he was recognized as a major figure in the government.
His rise was, as always, the result of a combination of intellect,
industry, and sociability. The Marquis de Chastellux, who
travelled extensively in America between 1780 and 1782, visited

Duane, who was then a member of the Philadelphia Congress, and found him "of a gay and open character, has no objection to talk, and drinks without repugnance."[16] Duane worked effectively with, and supported, Washington, Hamilton, Nathanael Greene, and John Jay, and successfully enough to provoke one observer to fume, "Whose friends fill all the high places? Mr. Duane's. Who are the treasury board? Mr. Duane's friends. Who are the admiralty board? Mr. Duane's friends. Who is financier? Mr. Duane's friend. In short, who puts up and puts down at his pleasure? Mr. Duane."[17] Despite such criticism, the "cautious and smooth Mr. Duane" impressed many with his "good and even temper, his attention to business, his low soft voice, not eloquent, nor designing, but upon the whole a good republican, desirous of promoting the general weal and particularly attached to the Interests of his own State."[18]

Surely, the new mayor brought experience to office. He would need it. Concerns over dislocation and redirection were evident. Much of the City was impoverished and the unemployed poor were a special problem. In August, 1784, Duane charged the Grand Jury of Quarter Sessions to investigate riots and disorders in the South Ward caused by the "vicious and abandoned." He promised a "school for the reformation of manners."[19] Five persons were sentenced to death by the court in a single day for robbery and burglary. William Mason was branded with a "T" on his left thumb for receiving a gold watch stolen from Duane. One observer noted in 1786 that he had never seen less energetic police than in New York. The Spanish Minister, Don Gardoqui, on the other hand, complimented New Yorkers and Duane on the fact that nothing was stolen during a fire at the Spanish legation.[20]

Duane, who sat as chief magistrate of the mayor's court, had at least one landmark case tried before him—*Rutgers v. Waddington* in 1784. Though Duane had suffered heavy property damage in the city and had risked a sizable fortune by joining the patriot cause, he had none of the bitterness toward the loyalists that characterized the political conduct of the more extreme Whigs. The memories of the Revolutionary War had split the community into hostile factions. In response to popular agitation, the state had passed a series of statutes destructive of civil and political rights of loyalists in derogation of the sixth article of the Treaty of Peace with England. Among these was the notorious Trespass Act of 1783. This legislation allowed Whigs (loyal Americans) who had fled from the British to bring suit against loyalists for trespass and damage to their real or personal property held behind British lines during the war. The act deprived the defendants of the right to offer as justification any military order or command of the enemy for the occupation or destruction of the property, and held that if suit were brought in any inferior court, it was to be therein finally determined. It was a "Tory-baiting" act aimed at limiting the political opposition to the new "Republican" government of George Clinton.

The case heard by Duane involved Joshua Waddington and Co., merchants, who had taken over the abandoned brewery of Elizabeth Rutgers, a widow, under a license of the British commissary general from 1778 to 1780 and, from 1780 to 1783, under orders of the British military authorities. Mrs. Rutgers fled the City when the British arrived in September 1776. When Waddington refused to reimburse Mrs. Rutgers for rent for the entire period of the war, she sued for redress under the Trespass Act. This was considered a test case; its outcome would determine the large number of pending cases of a similar nature. Attorney General Egbert Benson, assisted by several lawyers, including Robert Troup, represented the widow. Alexander Hamilton, Brockholst Livingston, and Morgan Lewis appeared for the wealthy but unpopular Waddington. The issue was clear. The prosecution argued that the state was sovereign within its borders, while the defendant argued for the rights of captives under international law and an amnesty to loyalists under the terms of the peace treaty with England of 1783. That treaty, Hamilton stated, was superior to state law.

Duane's decision was a political one. He avoided the issue. He straddled the major question—was an act of the legislature valid despite an international treaty obligation? Duane felt that the enactment of the legislature, even if unreasonable, could not be set aside by a court. Surely, the legislature did not intend to contradict the law of nations which the state constitution had adopted as part of its common law. Nevertheless, Duane held that the widow could collect damages for the time her property was held under the commissary general because the commissary general acted beyond his authority and that in the period under his license the brewery was not used "for the carrying on of the war" according to the terms of the statute. In allowing damages for the period 1778–1780, it appears that he was really making concessions to popular sentiment in favor of widow Rutgers. But for the period 1780–1783, when defendant had occupied the property under license from the British commander in chief, (who acted under the law of nations governing belligerents, when issuing his orders regarding the brewhouse) there would be no damages.

The compromise decision found little favor with Duane's opposition. Duane, writing to Washington, felt he had "lost credit with an Assembly though I hope not with the world." Washington replied that "reason seems very much in favor of the opinion of the court, and my judgment yields a hearty assent to it."[21] Radical Whigs sought to have all future mayoral appointments go to persons who would govern themselves by the "known laws of the land."[22]

For conservatives like Duane and Richard Varick, who would succeed Duane as mayor, the case was a bulwark against a "mob" element of radical democrats seeking to frighten and bully men of property. It would keep New York safe from those who thought the Revolution was more than a war for independence. Ultimately, the influence of the moderates brought about the modification of anti-Tory legislation. The Trespass Act was entirely repealed in 1788.

With the War for Independence over, the new nation looked expectantly to the future. There was excitement and a feeling of elation everywhere, but perhaps nowhere more than in New York City which only now was emerging from years of British occupation and hardship. The city had special reason to feel a sense of civic pride. In 1784, the ship *Empress of China* had left New York and for the first time carried the American flag across the Pacific opening a very lucrative and important Far-Eastern trade. The next year the *Experiment* duplicated the voyage and other ships followed in ever-growing number.

Also in 1784, the City's first banking institution, the Bank of New York was chartered, spurring the accumulation of investment capital. New York was also the site of many sessions of the Continental Congress. Leaders of the country, Rufus King, Franklin, and Washington, met with members of the social and political aristocracy of New York, including Robert R. Livingston, John Jay, William S. Smith, and Alexander Hamilton, and with the ministers of foreign countries—Don Diego Gardoqui of Spain, Peter Van Berckel of The Netherlands, and Barbé Marbois, French charge d'affaires.

The city, then as now, provided entertainment for visitors, but also had its share of critics. Governor William Livingston of New Jersey wrote in 1787 in reproof of New York's extravagance, "My principal secretary of state, who is one of my daughters is gone to New York to shake her heels at the balls and assemblies of the metropolis which might as well be more studious of paying its taxes than of instituting expensive diversions."[23] For the mayor, such sober thoughts were fleeting as he and his wife Mary attended to one of the duties of office— that of official greeter, host to the visitors to his fair city. This was a more cheerful burden of office.

As always, New York was a fashion center. The aristocratic part of the population, especially its women, dressed in the latest English pattern. "In the dress of its women," wrote a French observer, "you will see the most brilliant silks, gauzes, hats and borrowed hair. Equipages are rare; but they are elegant. The men have more simplicity in their dress; they disdain gewgaws, but they take their revenge in the delicacies of the table. Luxury forms already in this town a class of men very dangerous in society—I mean bachelors; the expense of women causes matrimony to be dreaded by men."[24]

The same observer, while delighting in the general atmosphere in New York, found the cost of living higher than almost anywhere else in the United States or in France. It would seem that some things have not changed over the years. John Adams found the city lacking in breeding and manners. "At their entertainments there is no conversation that is agreeable. . .they talk very loud, very fast, and all together."[25]

The enlightened social climate, the grand dinner parties, overshadowed the complaints of critics. Public and private parties all but swept up Mayor Duane and his coterie in the frenzy of preparing for the city's greatest events. It would host the inauguration of the nation's first president and celebrate the adoption of the United States Constitution. In what was probably New York's first "ticker-tape" parade, those in the city who supported ratification of the Constitution crowded the streets on Monday, July 23, 1788. The eleborate proceedings were arranged by Major Pierre L'Enfant, who would soon supervise the improvement to City Hall and later design the "Plan of the City of Washington."

A large procession composed of merchants, lawyers, doctors, clergymen, coopers, carpenters, coachmakers, and printers was organized. Upholsterers prepared a chair of state for the first president and the coachmakers crafted a "superb chariot." The most eye-catching objects in the parade were models of the Federal ships "Hamilton" and "Constitution," each carried by dozens of sailors. The procession started in the "Fields" or the "Common," the present site of City Hall Park, moved down Broadway and Whitehall Street, went up Pearl Street and ended at what we now know as Grand Street and Broadway. There a large pavilion had been erected, topped by a figure of *Fame* holding her trumpet ready to announce a new era to the world.

Mayor Duane had special reason to be proud of the event. He was a staunch supporter of strong national government and felt such government was necessary to protect liberty. A government without strength and authority "is food for the mob" and with that the end of property and liberty. Duane had played an important role at the Poughkeepsie convention that ratified the Constitution. In a speech to that assembly, he reminded his audience of the "melancholy experience" of the last war, which could have been lessened if a strong national government had been in effect. On July 26, 1788, the vote in favor of ratification was 30 to 27. The yeas included Duane.

Duane's concern with the power of mobs was reenforced by his experience of the so-called "Doctor's Riot" of April 1788. Caused largely by popular discontent with dissection and the practice of robbing fresh graves to provide cadavers for medical classes, the riot was touched off by the carelessness of a medical student in Dr. Richard Bayley's anatomy class. An outraged crowd stormed Columbia College and other buildings including New York Hospital. Duane finally resorted to the use of regular troops to restore order. Five people were killed and many others wounded.

By the end of March 1789, the first federal Congress met for business, mob or no mob, in a refurbished City Hall, renamed Federal Hall, the first United States Capitol. All awaited the arrival of George Washington. The old City Hall at the corner of Wall and Broad Streets, where the nineteenth-century custom-house now stands, had been given by the city to the new federal government to be used as its first and hopefully permanent capitol. This building had previously housed sessions of the provincial Assembly, supreme court, admiralty court, mayor's court and had served in part as a public library. The famous John Peter Zenger trial of 1735 had been conducted there in its spacious main courtroom. The old building had seen a great deal of history.

After a triumphant trip from his Mount Vernon home, president-elect Washington arrived in New York City on April 23, 1789, having been rowed, along with Richard Varick and Chancellor Robert R. Livingston, across the Hudson River in a magnificently decorated barge. Manned by thirteen master pilots, the barge arrived at Murray's Wharf, before a cheering crowd of government dignitaries and citizens, where Washington and his escort climbed the specially-carpeted ferry stairs. Declining the offer of a carriage, Washington walked through the city—accompanied by militia, members of Congress, Governor Clinton, Mayor Duane, members of the City Council, clergymen, and an entourage of French and Spanish ministers, followed by a large crowd of onlookers.

On Thursday, April 30, Washington marched again in another "Grand Procession" to Federal Hall for his inauguration. On a crowded balcony, overlooking a mass of citizens, Chancellor Livingston administered the oath of office. The country welcomed its first president, with shouts of joy and jubilation and the guns of the Battery boomed. New York and the nation belonged to the president. To cap the festivities, an inauguration ball was given at the city assembly rooms on the east side of Broadway, a little above Wall Street, on the evening of May 7, 1789. Invited dignitaries came to honor the president and his wife. For those who attended it was a most memorable occasion.[26]

Those incredible days of "Washington's New York" have rarely been equalled. Over the years there were many ceremonies, balls and parades, but very few, if any, matched the splendor of that of 1789. For the mayors of the city, festivities were and are part of the job, but few have equalled the experience of James Duane. City affairs, however, were only part of Duane's diversified interests. In 1782–1785 and 1788–1790, as a state senator he was an important participant in the politics of the commonwealth and a leading figure in the Federalist ranks. On many occasions his statesmanship rose above partisan considerations, for problems of state were not Duane's sole preoccupation. He was active in private business affairs, family matters, and the administration of his vast property west of Albany at Duanesburg. He set an excellent example for service in the cultural and philanthropic life of the City. In 1784, Duane, along with Robert Troup and others, became, by virtue of a new state charter for Trinity Church, a churchwarden with vestry power to induct a rector. In that year, Duane took part in the national reorganization of the Episcopal Church. He was a governor of the New York Hospital and vice president of the Society for the Relief of Distressed Debtors. In 1790, when streets were laid out on Trinity lands bordering the Hudson River, the first was named for Duane, to be followed by those named for vestrymen Jay, Harrison, Provoost, and others.[27]

Duane, one of New York's ruling aristocracy, had acquired in 1761 large tracts of land, including one which became his manor at Duanesburg in present-day Schenectady County. In the same year, he also acquired "Gramercy," that name being a corruption of the Dutch name, *Kroom Messie* (crooked little knife), given to a creek which ran through the land. This land was purchased from Gerradus Stuyvesant, grandson of Peter Stuyvesant. It lay on the east side of Bouwerie Road (now Third Avenue) some two-and-a-half miles from the center of New York. The present privately maintained Gramercy Park was part of the Duane purchase. Duane, like the Astors and Lenoxes, surely realized the potential of urban investment.

Duane, closely associated with King's College (now Columbia), was elected to its board of governors in 1762, eight years after its founding. In January 1784, as state senator, he headed a committee whose work resulted in the creation of the University of the State of New York with Columbia College as its leading institution. Duane's work as chairman of the state's regents led to the separation of Columbia from the state university system and to an emphasis on the development of public education. He was later elected chairman of the Columbia Board of Trustees. In May 1789, he proudly heard his son James deliver the salutatory address on the study of philosophy and mathematics at Columbia's graduation ceremony, where President Washington and Vice-President John Adams were among the distinguished audience. In 1792, the University of Edinburgh conferred the degree of Doctor of Law upon Duane, Varick, and Jay in recognition of their achievements in the fields of law and education.

Though Trinity and Columbia occupied most of his time outside of his mayoral duties, in 1785 Duane became an original member of the Society in Promoting the Manumission of Slaves and contributed money to a number of societies promoting humanitarianism. He was an honorary member of the Society of Cincinnati, a group composed of Revolutionary War officers, and nearly every March 17 found him celebrating with other "Friendly Sons of St. Patrick." [28]

Duane received recognition for his long labors on behalf of the nation when in 1789, Washington appointed him to be the first judge of the Federal District Court of New York. The press of official duties compelled Duane to resign from his posts as state senator and mayor. The new position was as financially rewarding as the post of mayor and allowed him to spend more leisure time at Duanesburg. Duane received £600 per year as a judge. While mayor, Duane received fees from a number of sources: clerk of the market, revenue from tavern licenses, and certificates issued for freemen, cartmen, and butchers and incidental perquisites from acknowledging deeds, bail pieces, and taxing lists. Duane in this way earned from £700 to £800 per year. [29]

As federal judge, Duane heard a number of significant cases, including two in 1793 involving the treaty with France of 1788 which allowed the French to bring prizes into American ports. Duane held that the taking of captives within neutral American waters was illegal and ordered such prisoners released. The French consul protested, but to no avail.

On March 10, 1794, Duane wrote to President Washington to report that he suffered a stomach disorder contracted by lack of "regular exercise" and "relaxation" and asked to be retired from office. Reluctantly, Washington agreed and Duane returned to Duanesburg with his family, leaving their rented house at 17 Nassau Street and their home at Gramercy. Duane soon became a country squire tending to land rentals at Duanesburg.

James Duane died on February 1, 1797. A memorial in the churchyard at Duanesburg reads in part: "The Honorable James Duane Esquire whose remains here rest, . . . Earnest at the Bar, Enlightened and Impartial as a Judge: to the Knowledge of a Statesman the Manners of a Gentleman who joined; and all the

Domestic Virtues, the Social Affections were his. . . His Widowed Partner has Erected this Monument, due to his Worth, to her Affection, and Her Grief.''[30]

The Varick Years, 1789–1801

On September 20, 1789, Governor George Clinton replaced retiring Mayor James Duane with another ardent Federalist, Richard Varick. ''Conservative in temperament, staunchly Federalist in politics—Varick was hardly the sort to approve of the vast political changes that were to take place in the city during his incumbency.''[31] He took office on October 14, 1789. Both the Duane and Varick appointments broadened the political support for conservatives increasingly identified with merchants and bankers supporting Alexander Hamilton, and perhaps weakened Clinton's Democratic-Republican party identified with small tenants, farmers, and artisans. Whatever motive Clinton may have had in naming Varick, the appointment, like that of Duane, went to a member of the aristocracy.

As with Duane and so many others in non-elected public service at the time, Varick came from an established, if not too well-known, Dutch family, originally Van Varick. He was born in Hackensack, New Jersey, on March 25, 1753, and graduated from King's College. (Later in life he was to become a trustee of that institution.) He studied law, and at twenty-one began a practice which was interrupted by the outbreak of the Revolution. He aided the patriot cause and began a promising military career as a captain in Colonel Alexander McDougall's First New York Continental Regiment.

He subsequently served as military secretary to General Philip Schuyler, who recommended that Varick be appointed deputy muster master, a suggestion adopted by Congress in September 1776. Varick was given the rank of lieutenant colonel on April 10, 1777, and remained with the northern army until the Muster Department was abolished after the capture of General Burgoyne in October 1777. He participated in the battles of Stillwater and Saratoga, and, after 1780, became inspector-general at West Point and first aide-de-camp, or military secretary, to General Benedict Arnold, whom he admired as a soldier. When

Arnold defected to the British, a story circulated to the effect that Varick had some involvement in the plot. Certain of his innocence, he petitioned Washington for a court of inquiry which met on November 4 and 5, 1780, and acquitted him with honor.[32] Despite the verdict, Varick remained under suspicion. In November 1780, he wrote to Washington explaining that the abolition of the Muster Department and Arnold's treason had left him stranded and he asked Washington to speak to Congress on his behalf. Washington received approval from Congress to appoint a confidential secretary and staff of writers to record his letters. In 1781, General Washington selected Varick as his recording secretary and Varick's integrity was established. Washington assigned him to compile a record of his papers, a task not completed until 1783.[33]

Varick had looked forward to resuming his legal practice, but again public service interfered. Well over six feet tall, Varick had an imposing presence; "a severe magistrate, an upright and honorable man, somewhat austere and lofty in his manner, but humane and charitable in his disposition and conduct," and adapted well to the many posts offered him. He was appointed recorder of the city in February 1784 by Governor Clinton. In a letter of congratulations, Mayor Duane pointed out that "however disadvantageous it may prove to your profession," the position was "an honorable testimony of your patriotism and integrity."

As city recorder from 1784 until his resignation in 1789, Varick was a conscientious and industrious public official. He became an ardent watchman of the public treasury, careful to see that city government was not abused by self-serving politicians. For example, in 1788 he successfully urged the removal of a city surveyor, arguing that it was a conflict of interest for a man who regulated the streets in an official capacity to pursue, at the same time, the trade of a mason. Varick also served as a member of the Assembly, was speaker in 1787 and 1788, and along with Samuel Jones, Sr., prepared a codification of colonial statutes, a task completed in 1789. Jones succeeded Varick as recorder. Varick served as state attorney-general in 1788–89.[34]

It was during this busy political time in his life that Varick in 1786 married Maria Roosevelt, which signalled his entrance into fashionable society. Varick was also an elder in the Dutch Reformed Church and very active in his congregation.

This vignette portrait of Richard Varick was published in James Grant Wilson's Memorial History of the City of New-York.

It was in 1790, during his administration, that New York City's brief career as the first national capital under the Constitution came to an end with the closing of the second session of the First Congress on August 12, 1790. New Yorkers had welcomed the new nation and delighted in their city's designation as the capital. Its citizens saw signs of a bountiful future. The loss of the capital for some was an ominous sign that the city would become "a wilderness again, peopled with wolves its old inhabitants." Others looked forward to simpler times and a return "to our old principles of honest Dutch economy and plain New York hospitality."[35]

During Varick's administration, two court cases caused tremendous political agitation in the city. The first involved ferry service to Brooklyn. In November 1795, two ferrymen, both recently arrived Irish immigrants, Timothy Crady and Thomas Burk, became involved in a dispute with Alderman Gabrial Furman, who had charged them with insulting him and threatening High Constable James Culbertson. Both ferrymen were confined to Bridewell Prison where they were held for twelve days before being brought to trial in the court of general sessions. Varick sat as judge. The trial raised the question of the quality of the ferry service which, it was argued, was run by "strangers ignorant of their duty," often intoxicated and abusive to passengers. Crady was given twenty lashes on his bare back and two months in prison. Burk was given two months in prison. The affair led to allegations of "tyrannical" and vindictive attitudes toward the Irish, especially by the mayor.

The second case involved the *Thetis*, a British frigate. City magistrates were accused of having imprisoned nine deserters from the *Thetis* and then voluntarily sending them back to the ship. Popular outcry demanded an investigation of this matter and of the Burk-Crady affair as well. During the *Thetis* incident Crady escaped from prison and subsequently died—cause unknown. The *New York Journal* insinuated that the death might have been caused by the twenty lashes the ferryman had received. Because of these occurrences, anti-British and anti-Varick feelings were inflamed and directed basically toward the Federalists. A grand jury conducted an investigation and reported to the state supreme court on January 29, 1796 that the proceedings in the Burk-Crady affair were correct. In addition, the jury reported that the nine sailors had voluntarily returned to the *Thetis*. Though cleared of all charges, Varick remained under public suspicion, especially by those of anti-Federalist persuasion.

Burk retained Alexander Hamilton to bring suit against Varick and several other magistrates for "cruelty and injustice." Varick and his fellow officials were arrested. A few days before the trial in the supreme court, the suit was settled for £500. Varick evidently thought this an acceptable price to pay to free himself from a hornet's nest and possible further damage to his political career.[36]

Conflict came with the office of mayor. As a staunch Federalist, Varick was often in the center of political power-brokering. In 1792, he suspended the granting of freemanships to cartmen, inn-keepers, and others who were seemingly not friends and fellow partisans. Democratic-Republicans used this as an example of Federalist tyranny and misuse of office.

Politics may have been a major preoccupation of New Yorkers —the question of clean wharves, clean streets and public health was another. In 1786, while Recorder, Varick received a letter from an irate citizen complaining of dirty streets and wharves which he felt caused dreaded "malignant fevers." He denounced Varick as a "scoundrel, rascal, and detestable miscreant" for not taking adequate steps to clean the city. During Varick's mayoralty, disease and sanitation problems reached major proportions. In the 1790s, yellow fever epidemics occurred almost annually, culminating with the terrible plague of 1798, in which thousands perished. This epidemic prompted the common council to take radical measures to combat the illness. A committee was appointed to investigate the causes of the "Pestilential Disease." The committee attributed the persistence of epidemics to the presence of "filthy sunken yards filled with offals of the house and wash of the kitchen" which emptied into rivers or ponds. In addition, the "lack of a plentiful supply of fresh water" added to the severity of the disease. Recurring yellow fever epidemics, especially those of 1795 and 1798, not only spurned activity meant to clean the city, but emphasized the need for an adequate water supply.[37] This problem had long concerned the city and by the Revolution only a very few wells, notably the Tea Water Pump on Chatham Street (now Park Row) near present Chatham Square, could be used for drinking purposes. Even that water was suspect as the nearby Fresh Water Pond (the Collect) was used even before the war as a common sewer, and all manner of waste, including dead dogs and cats, was thrown in daily.

In 1774, Christopher Colles with common council approval had begun construction of a reservoir system that included the use of underground wooden water pipes, but the project was abandoned during the war. On April 2, 1799, the state legislature, at the urging of Aaron Burr, John Murray, president of the chamber of commerce, Gulian Verplanck, president of the New York branch of the Bank of the United States, and Alexander Hamilton, passed a bill creating the Manhattan Company to supply the City with "pure and wholesome water." It was a private company with the City allowed to subscribe. In 1800, a reservoir was built on the north side of Chambers Street and soon some 400 houses were supplied with water. It was only a temporary solution, but a start had been made.

The act that created the water company also created a bank, which with the help of Aaron Burr, was included in the fine print of the act. This was the second bank founded in New York, The Bank of the Manhattan Company. The first such institution, as has been noted, was created in 1784 as the Bank of New York. Incorporated in 1791, with aid from Alexander Hamilton, the bank was directed from 1792 to 1794 by Mayor Varick, who held seven shares of the bank's stock.[38]

Additional laws were enacted to address matters relating to public health, including creation of a special street cleaning department which significantly lessened the city's sanitation problem. Concern about contagion, filth, and lack of adequate medical facilities led some of New York's leading physicians such as Richard Bayley and Samuel Bard to create additional hospital space as well as better care for the poor. Their efforts resulted in the building of a new almshouse on the north side of Chambers Street in 1796. Two years later, the city purchased a five-acre estate, Belle Vue, from attorney Brockholst Livingston to isolate persons having malignant fever. A board of health was authorized to supervise the city's medical concerns.[39]

Complexities of city government evolved at every level. Patronage at the mayor's command was considerable, adding to the burden as well as the emoluments of office. Records from 1789 to 1797 reveal that the mayor appointed the high constable, chief marshall, deputy market clerk, sealers and markers, water bailiff and forty-eight deputy marshals, thirty-five scavengers, thirty-one porters, and over a thousand cartmen. Like Duane, Varick received no salary, earning his income essentially from fees—especially from the licensing of taverns.[40]

Taverns were important to the social fabric of the City and served many functions. For political purposes, the taverns were invaluable. Before 1790, a tavern in each ward served as a polling place. People who had similar political views frequented certain taverns where the latest news was exchanged. Business transactions took place at these convenient places and ship news, price lists, and other economic information was available. In 1793, the newly-built Tontine Coffee House on Wall Street became stock exchange headquarters. For social purposes, taverns were ideal, especially as a meeting place for clubs and societies.

Part of the mayor's salary was, as has been mentioned, derived from certificates issued to newly-inducted freemen, marshals, cartmen and butchers. Funds derived from issuance of these licenses were cause of much criticism and the city council attempted to control the practice. In 1790, the mayor's allowance was set at £700 per year in addition to fees from licenses issued to marshals, cartmen, and butchers. Tavern and market license fees were omitted. Varick was granted a salary of £1000 in 1795 and £1415 in 1800. Although Varick cooperated with the council in reducing his fees, Democratic-Republican writers attacked him on the tavern license and market issue. Varick defended his position, but to little avail.[41] In 1813, a fixed salary was voted the mayor and the fee and license system was abolished.

During George Washington's first administration, party or factional politics emerged to dominate the early years of the Republic. Hopes to have the new nation free from such strife were, despite the Constitution and Washington, doomed to defeat. Nowhere was the struggle for power more naked than in New York City. In no community were political careers so short or so unsuccessful in gaining national honor. Careers were lost in combat between Federalists and Republicans. In New York City, politics was not a springboard to glory, but a call to early retirement.

Political conflicts were waged in the streets. New Yorkers learned to take sides quickly and often. The French Revolution, which began just a few weeks after Washington first took office, was generally welcomed everywhere in America. In 1790, when Marquis de Lafayette sent Washington the key to the Bastille, the president acknowledged it as a "token of victory gained by liberty over despotism." However, the excesses of the Revolution changed public opinion. Most Americans were horrified by the Jacobin Reign of Terror. French wars against the continental monarchs and ensuing executions helped rally conservative (Federalist) opinion against France. The Jeffersonians, supported by the newly created St. Tammany Society (1786), despised monarchy and voiced their confidence in the French people. Washington insisted on a policy of neutrality. War in Europe, begun in 1792, created a great demand for American food and equipment. Neutral maritime nations like the United States benefited. Britain, a belligerent power, decreed that all shipping to and from France and French colonies would be subject to British search and possible seizure. The British in Canada chose this very time to arm and incite Indians to raid the Northwest Territory where thousands of Americans had settled. Furthermore, the British made it clear that they had no intention of relinquishing their armed posts on American territory until terms of the peace treaty of 1783, especially those relating to Tory seizures, were met. The issues of trade and territory forced a Republican embargo through Congress in 1794. This embargo kept British ships out of American ports and seriously impaired the trade of merchants, a majority of whom were Federalists.

On April 16, 1794, Washington appointed Chief Justice John Jay to go to England as a special envoy and settle the main differences between both countries. The Treaty of London, known in America as Jay's Treaty, was extremely unsatisfactory. The British agreed to evacuate their posts in the Northwest, but according to the terms of the treaty, could still engage in fur trapping on the American side of the Canadian border. In addition, they could still trade with the Indians who were hostile to American settlements. These concessions almost nullified England's surrender of the posts. The treaty contained nothing that would deter the British from stopping and searching all American ships on the seas. Nor did the treaty halt the British practice of impressing American crews at will. The British argued that men so taken were, in fact, deserters. Finally, the treaty left to the British the privilege of defining contraband goods. The most objectionable arrangement in the treaty was that in exchange for the privilege of trading with the British West Indies, Jay agreed that all American cargoes of molasses, coffee, cocoa, sugar, and cotton (the only valuable British West Indies commodities) must be carried directly to American ports. Trade in these commodities, beyond America, was denied to American merchants, but British ships could carry them anywhere in the world, including American ports. As the public became aware of the terms of the treaty, their response was violent, and nowhere more so than in New York City.

Jay's task had been difficult and delicate and he surely achieved as much and more by way of concessions than would have been expected. He was not, however, greeted by a cheering public. He was burnt in effigy in Philadelphia and New York City for having sold his country for British gold. At a mass meeting held in July 1795 in front of City Hall, both Mayor Varick and Hamilton attempted to defend the treaty but they and presiding officer Edward Livingston were unsuccessful and the meeting ended in near riot. Later, Hamilton tried to talk to a crowd of people in front of his home on the corner of Wall and Broad Streets, but stones were thrown, one striking him in the head. He was said to have observed, "By your use of such striking arguments, I must retire." The screaming crowd proceeded to Bowling Green where they burned copies of the treaty and raised the French flag. Still, the Chamber of Commerce approved of the treaty, as did many New Yorkers.

Jay, while in England, was elected governor of New York. He arrived in New York City on May 28, 1795 and was inaugurated in July 1, 1795.[42] The treaty was finally approved by the United States Senate on June 25, 1795, by a two-thirds majority. The House of Representatives voted appropriations under the agreement by a vote of 51 to 48. A possible war with England had been averted by three votes.

The Jay Treaty crisis and the deterioration of relations with France following the 1793 Genet affair (in which Edmond Genet, in a tactless endeavor to gain support for the French Revolution, involved himself in American politics, and created anti-French popular sentiment) stimulated a popular effort to strengthen the defenses of New York harbor. The work was effected largely by citizens of the city in voluntary association.

This was noted by a visiting and admiring Englishman, who saw "A patriotic and general resolution of the inhabitants of this city, to work a day gratis, without distinction of rank or condition, for the public advantage, on these fortifications." Each day came carpenters, teachers, lawyers, coopers, all united by love of country, all at work firming the social compact. New Yorkers had their quarrels and partisan politics in abundance, but they also could associate themselves in common cause and social harmony.[43]

New York's first theatre, The New Theatre, was opened late in 1732 and joined by a second on Nassau Street by 1750. But local artistry was limited and New York was dependent on the English stage for plays and for such actors as William and Lewis Hallam (father and son). As a result, with the British evacuation New York lost most of its professional performers. The John Street Theatre, founded in 1767, enjoyed a revival with the return of Lewis Hallam in 1785. With the opening in 1798 under the direction of William Dunlap of the Park Theatre on present-day Park Row (then Chatham Street), the first theatre in the post-war period, the start of a new era, an American era was begun. It was a fitting tribute to the vitality and potential of the city, something perhaps not appreciated by those leaving for the new capital, Albany. The new building was an impressive structure designed by Joseph Mangin, a French architect, who, with John McComb, would very shortly submit a design for the City Hall that still serves New York City. The Park led to the building of other theatres and the immediate area of canvas tents and the poorhouse was transformed into a valuable residential business as well as a political center.[44]

There were many other examples of cultural progress, King's College (founded in 1754) became Columbia in 1784. The curriculum was enlarged as were the number of students in attendance. In 1791 medical teaching was revived and in 1792 Dr. Samuel Bard became dean of a newly founded medical department. James Kent began lecturing as professor of law in 1793 and Dr. Samuel L. Mitchell taught natural history and chemistry. The first decade under the Constitution also saw a revival of other forms of intellectual life. Washington Irving formed the Calliopean Society in 1788 as a literary club, the *New Yorker Magazine*, published from 1790 to 1797, stimulated interest in art and helped Dr. Mitchell publish the *Medical Repository* in

1797 as the first of a long series of annual volumes, basically on medical history and affairs. It was the first and for a long time the only such journal in the country.

The publishing business flourished, as did libraries. Printed directories—David Frank's issue of 1786 was the first, and David Longworth continued the effort—were indicative of growth. Newspapers found a new surge of interest, and to the honor roll of American printers, such as William Bradford and John Zenger, could be added Francis Childs, whose *Daily Advertiser* of 1785 was the first daily in New York and third in the nation. Noah Webster began the *American Minerva* in 1793 which became the *Commercial Advertiser* in 1797. Samuel Loudon published the *Mercantile Advertiser* in 1798, while Charles Webster and John McLean started the *Daily Gazette* in 1788. In that same year, John and Archibald McLean published *The Federalist*, one of the most important political tracts in the nation's history. During this decade, New York also became a major center of art. It became home to John Trumbull, Charles Willson Peale, and John Vanderlyn. Duncan Phyfe, furniture maker, began his career in the city in 1790, joining other craftsmen, such as Thomas and William Ash. To meet the ever present need for housing, the City Hotel—the first of its kind—was built in 1794 on Broadway.

New York, despite its problems, was by the end of the century a tolerant city. The first Catholic church, St. Peter's, was built in 1785–86 at the corner of Barclay and Church Streets. The African Methodist Episcopalian Church held their first meeting in a school room on Frankfort Street in 1809, as blacks of the city struggled for a meaningful identity. After years of discussion involving the issue of abolition of slavery, the state legislature passed a bill initially suggested by members of the New York Manumission Society (organized in 1785, John Jay and Alexander Hamilton served as its first presidents; James Duane and Robert R. Livingston were founding members) which provided for the gradual manumission of all slaves beginning on July 4, 1799. The achievement of full civil rights remained to be accomplished.

There were, by 1800, some 60,000 in the city—people of all sorts. It was a bountiful city. One visitor, Moreau de St. Mery, commented that "extremely fat people are seen frequently. They are usually people of color, and for the most part women, and generally mulattoes."[45] It is little wonder that the girth of New Yorkers was eye-catching considering that there were four public markets. The Fly market at the foot of Maiden Lane was the largest, containing great quantities of meat, sixty-three sorts of fish in addition to a large variety of shellfish, fifty-one varieties of animal and game, a large assortment of vegetables, and all the ice cream one could want (it was made by French inhabitants).

Some thirty churches, including St. Peter's, and one synagogue served the spiritual need of the city's citizens. St. Paul's Chapel on Broadway was the loveliest. Trinity Episcopal Church, just below St. Paul's, also on Broadway facing Wall Street, was in 1798–1790 newly rebuilt, having burned in 1776. It was probably the largest and surely most prestigious of all churches.[46]

There were setbacks. New York's position as capital of the state was slowly eroded as offices and records were moved to Albany. Several factors influenced this relocation: New York City was vulnerable to attack, as its seizure by the British in 1776 demonstrated. In addition, the state's prinicpal leaders, such as Governor Clinton and Chancellor Robert R. Livingston lived as did many of its people, nearer to Albany than to New York. Convenience was thus a factor, as was, perhaps, the fact that the City was pestilence ridden, with problems of filth, crime, pauperism and riot. The Albany move may be seen as an early example of suburban exodus. Whatever the reason, in January 1798 the seat of government was installed in Albany, the present capital city.[47]

New York at the beginning of the nineteenth century was at the edge of greatness. Its past helped in preparing its future. It had recovered from occupation and the ravages of war; it had survived a critical period of social, political, and economic change. Its first mayors had helped in that transition. Their courses of action, like the Constitution during this time of testing, would serve oncoming generations.

Having served diligently every year since 1789, Mayor Richard Varick must have happily welcomed his successor, Edward Livingston, who became mayor on August 10, 1801. Varick resumed his legal career, joined the Federalist Washington Benevolent Society in 1809, and remained active in politics. Varick was also a member and a president of New York Society of the Cincinnati. He remained interested in the military and in the organization of the state militia and was appointed colonel of one of its regiments. For many years (1808–1820), he was also president of the Merchants Bank, the city's third such institution, and a founder and benefactor of the American Bible Society. After the war of 1812, his political interest subsided, though he was one of the appraisers for the Erie Canal. Often seen in the city, he had little to do with its affairs. He died at his residence, Prospect Point in Jersey City, on July 30, 1831, in his seventy-ninth year.

Notes

1. Ira Rosenwaike, *Population History of New York City* (Syracuse, 1972), 8, 9.
2. Virginia Harrington, *The New York Merchant on the Eve of the Revolution* (New York, 1935), 353.
3. Rosenwaike, *Population History*, 15.
4. Alexander C. Flick, *Loyalism in New York During the American Revolution* (New York, 1901), 171; See *New York Morning Post*, November 7, 1783 for a parody of "to be or not to be."
5. Sidney I. Pomerantz, *New York an American City* 1783–1803: *A Study of Urban Life* (New York, 1938), 69-70.
6. Edward P. Alexander, *A Revolutionary Conservative: James Duane of New York* (New York, 1938), 158.
7. New York City, *Minutes of the Common Council of 1784–1831* (New York, 1917–30), 1:14.
8. Alexander, *Duane*, 159.
9. Ibid., 21.
10. Ibid., 97.
11. Page Smith, *John Adams*, 2 vols. (New York, 1962), 1:164.
12. Alexander, *Duane*, 121.
13. Ibid., 120.
14. Ibid., 110.
15. Ibid., 132.
16. Howard C. Rice, Jr., *Travels in North America in the Years 1780, 1781 and 1782*, 2 vols. (Chapel Hill, 1963), 1:219.
17. Alexander, *Duane*, 145.
18. Ibid., 149-50.
19. Ibid., 160.
20. Ibid.
21. Ibid., 163.
22. Ibid., 162-164.
23. Rufus W. Griswold, *The Republican Court or American Society in the Days of Washington* (New York, 1856), 83–84.
24. Ibid., 87.
25. Smith, *John Adams*, 1:166.
26. Griswold, *Republican Court*, 113-145.
27. Alexander, *Duane*, 178-179, 186.
28. Ibid., 53–54, 185–186.

29. Pomerantz, *New York*, 39.

30. Ibid., 208–9, 213–236.

31. Pomerantz, *New York*, 108.

32. Albert B. Hart, *The Varick Court of Inquiry* (Boston, 1897), 47–48.

33. Pomerantz, *New York*, 43.

34. Ibid., 43, 108.

35. Ibid., 110.

36. Ibid., 264–7.

37. Valentine Seaman, *An Inquiry into the cause of the Prevalence of Yellow Fever in New York, The Medical Reporting* (New York, 1800), 119–131, 303–323.

38. Kenneth and Anne Roberts, eds., *Moreau de St. Mery's American Journey (1793–1798)* (New York, 1947), 147; Allen Nevins, *History of the Bank of New York and Trust Company 1784 to 1934* (New York, 1934), iii, xiii; Pomerantz, *New York*, 278–285.

39. Robert J. Carlisle, ed., *An Account of Bellevue Hospital* (New York, 1893), 9-13.

40. Pomerantz, *New York*, 44–45.

41. Ibid., 131.

42. James G. Wilson, *The Memorial History of the City of New York*, 5 vols. (New York, 1891–94), 3:125–128.

43. Henry Wansey, *The Journal of an Excursion to the United States of North America, in the Summer of 1794* (Salisbury, England, 1796), 83.

44. Mary C. Henderson, *The City and the Theatre* (Clifton, N.J., 1973), 13-50.

45. Roberts, *American Journey*, 149.

46. Ibid., 150, 231. See also Jonathan Greenlief, *A History of the Churches of all Denominations in the City of New York* (New York, 1846), 79, 334-35; Edgar J. McManus, *A History of Negro Slavery in New York* (Syracuse, N.Y.), 168, 174.

47. The controversy regarding the location of the state capital was so intense that the legislature did not explicitly designate Albany as the capital. Legislative acts merely established various state offices and buildings in Albany, and designated that city as the meeting place of the legislature. It was not until the 1980s that Albany was officially designated capital of New York State. See Albert B. Corey, "Your State Historian Speaking," *New York History* 27 (January 1946), 122–23.

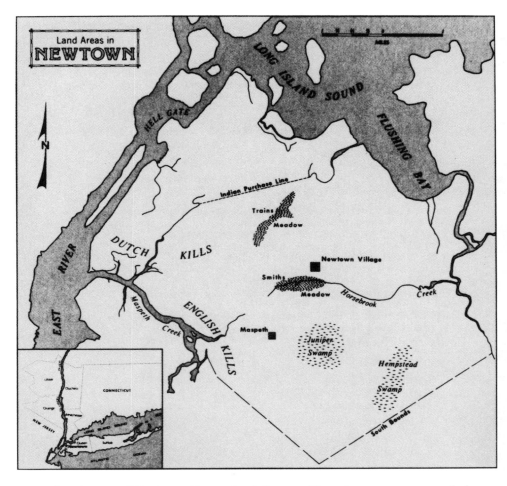

Land areas of Newtown. Drawn by J. Spencer Ulrey from sources compiled by Jessica Kross. From Kross, The Evolution of an American Town *(Temple University Press, 1983)*. © 1983 by Temple University. Reprinted by permission of Temple University Press.

Continuities and Change: Newtown, New York, 1777–1800

Jessica Kross

Any major military and political upheaval brings with it the potential for large-scale change. Newtown, a small farming village on western Long Island, was one of the first communities occupied by the British in 1776 and one of the last evacuated in 1783. Moreover, being close to New York City its inhabitants were aware of and affected by events in what would be America's busiest city. And yet the story told here will document more continuities than change; more evolution than revolution. Individuals undoubtedly had their lives altered in both positive and negative ways by the Revolution and the years immediately following it. But a community responds more slowly to shifts in demographic, economic and political structures. The independent Newtown of 1800 would have been easily recognizable to the loyal subjects of 1775.

Travellers to Long Island at the time of the American Revolution were pleased by what they saw. As one anonymous German officer, stationed in New York during the Revolution, noted, "Long-Island is a beautiful island. It has a great number of meadows, orchards, fruit-trees of all descriptions, and fine houses." He then described several of the villages, including Newtown. "Here are to be seen neat little houses surrounded by gardens, meadows and fruit-trees of every variety."[1]

The townsmen of western Long Island were primarily agriculturalists. They grew grains and vegetables, kept cattle and tended orchards. Their principal market was New York City, only a boat ride away from Brooklyn and six miles from Newtown by road and ferry. This proximity gave them what Edward Countryman has described as "automatic membership in the world of Atlantic commerce," a world reflected in the imported goods which appeared in probate inventories and account books. They also practiced some crafts. In Newtown there were blacksmiths, millers, weavers, shoemakers, cordwainers, and at various times schoolmasters.[2] Most males, judging from petitions, wills, and land records, were literate.

Long before the Revolution townsmen had carved up Newtown's 16,800 acres into private holdings and had already begun that exportation of sons which many New England towns experienced. A census of 1771 listed 189 households or roughly 1,100 whites. In 1756, there were 326 slaves. By the Battle of Long Island in 1776 probably some 1,600 whites and blacks inhabited the town.[3] In many ways, Newtown was Countryman's quintessential royalist village. It had a below average growth rate, yeoman freehold farming with a relatively narrow distance between the wealthiest and the poor, a history of social peace, and a prosperity based on "rising land values [and] closeness to market. . . ."[4] However, Newtown was not Tory; it would be, in fact, the most radical of the Queens County towns.

Newtown's farmers regulated themselves through the town officers elected yearly at the April town meeting. Appointed representatives to the general assembly, none of whom were from Newtown before the Revolution.[5] Unfortunately, no voting lists survive for Newtown from the colonial period. It is impossible to know whom the townsmen supported or how many voted. Until almost the eve of the Revolution they seemed to remain aloof from provincial or imperial concerns, although it is hard to agree with Edward Countryman that pre-Revolutionary townsmen felt themselves "unable to control their own lives, that greater men had to do it for them."[6] Instead, Newtowners shared the prevalent colonial attitude that less government was better.

The agitation of the mid-1770s would bring townsmen into the political fray and divide them. Reacting to a request from the Continental Congress that each town elect a committee of correspondence, on December 10, 1774, "a great number of the most respectable freeholders" chose a committee of seventeen. This committee included men who would later back out, such as the justices Richard Alsop and Daniel Rapalje, as well as those who would become active Revolutionaries like Jacob Blackwell and Samuel Riker. On December 29 the committee met and passed five resolutions which on the one hand confirmed allegiance to George III but on the other affirmed the colonists' right to dispose of their own property, i.e., no taxation without representation. Their fifth resolve commended the Continental Congress while identifying themselves as "freeborn Englishmen" within the British empire.[7]

Reaction soon followed. By January 1775 fifty-six townsmen protested against both these resolves and the Continental Congress itself. Four months later, 100 townsmen voted to send Jacob Blackwell, who would become a prominent Whig-in-exile, to a provincial convention assembled to elect delegates to the Second Continental Congress. An indication of the divisions within the town is that only five names appeared on both lists. As it turned out, only Newtown and Flushing agreed to participate in this process and Queens County gained a wide-spread reputation for loyalism.[8]

Although first moves in the Revolution favored the patriots at the expense of their Tory neighbors, both groups soon experienced the beginning of what would be a seven-year struggle to retain both dignity and property. In January 1776 the Continental Congress ordered Colonel Nathaniel Heard, at the head of 500 New Jersey militiamen, to disarm Queens County Tories and arrest those refusing to follow the resolutions of Congress. In June they authorized George Washington to remove loyalist prisoners from the county. Fearing an imminent British invasion, Congress also ordered all livestock removed to either the north shore or to Suffolk County. The task was not completed before the British invasion in late August, and a German officer commented, weeks later, that "Cattle are still to be found in large numbers, notwithstanding the immense droves which the rebels carried off with them on their retreat."[9]

The Battle of Long Island, which began on August 22, 1776, ended on August 30 with a complete rout of the Americans. The British army settled in and began an occupation of western Long Island which terminated only when the British left America for good on December 4, 1783.[10]

Even before the British invasion, civil government in New York was crumbling as Whigs and loyalists jockeyed for power. Royal government still existed but parallel to it were the various provincial conventions which claimed to have popular backing.

When elections in January 1776 produced an overwhelmingly Whig Assembly, whose members included Newtown's Jacob Blackwell, Governor William Tryon prorogued them, and this Assembly never met; British control over a unified province was at an end.[11] Lower New York would soon find itself under military government. The rest of the state was governed by a provincial congress which now had to coordinate a war effort, protect itself from enemies within, and try to establish some form of political legitimacy.

The Fourth Provincial Congress, the first to meet after independence was officially declared, restyled itself the Convention of Representatives of the State of New York and determined to write a state constitution. Among those making the decision were delegates from the occupied counties of lower New York, including New York, Kings and Queens. A number of these delegates sat on the committee drafting the constitution, but they were, in effect, Whigs in exile who would have to wait for the war's end to return to their homes. On April 20, 1777, thirty-three of the convention's thirty-four members present approved the constitution and on September 10 the new legislature met for the first time. Unoccupied New York was now an independent state.[12]

Political decisions made in the new state legislature would mean little to Newtown, which the British occupied until the end of the war. Rights and privileges conferred by the 1777 constitution would also have to wait. In the meantime, the town would try to carry on a normal life under abnormal conditions.

The American defeat in the Battle of Long Island immediately affected Newtown's population. Mistreatment of loyalists before the British occupation meant that little sympathy would be accorded to rabid Whigs. Some of these men left, although a few would return before the end of the war. Colonel Jacob Blackwell and Major Jonathan Lawrence would both sit in the third and fourth provincial congress. Blackwell, however, would return to Newtown sometime before the end of the war while Lawrence went to Rhinebeck in Dutchess county. Others of the old town elite would also leave. Dr. Joseph Sackett, a physician, went into the American army. The Reverend Simon Horton and his son-in-law Captain Benjamin Coe moved to Warwick, Orange County.[13]

Not all who left town were the well-established. Some, like

Nathan Furman, who was twenty-two in 1776, joined the army. Years later, Furman stated, "When Sir William Howe's fleet and army arrived at the Narrows and took possession of Staten Island there was a call for every fourth man to arm and take the field." He became a volunteer in Colonel Smith's regiment in June or early July, 1776. Furman was eventually taken prisoner and jailed in New York City. With the help of friends and relatives he escaped. Some eight months after joining the army he made his way back home, resided with his father and married in Newtown. He would remain in town until 1796 when he and his family moved to Orange County.[14]

On the other hand, Garrett Remson, born in 1749, was an artificer throughout the war. As General Jeremiah Johnson later noted in his affidavit to the commissioner of pensions:

> I knew Garret Remsen from 1776 and was at his father-in-laws house at Newtown the day after the Battle of Long Island he came in his trooper's uniform, fatigued and lay down to rest. He was not there an hour when a Tory named James Marr with a file of British soldiers came to take him. They failed and after they left he left....He left Long Island...and joined the American army and remained an exile until the British left the country when he returned he was poor and his farm ruined by the tories and refugees.[15]

It is difficult to determine how many left Newtown during the war. Various secondary sources, genealogies, the Revolutionary War Pension Records and lists of derelict property show that between twenty-six and thirty-six men left the town, either as refugees or soldiers. If the adult white male population of Newtown was somewhere around 225 in 1775, then 12 percent to 16 percent of adult white males left the town, at least temporarily. However, there seems to have been some permeability in the line between exiles and residents when even highly placed former Whigs, like Jacob Blackwell, could return to a presumably non-political quiet life.[16]

Of greater effect upon town life was the arrival of those persons who came as a result of the British occupation. Newcomers included both civilians and soldiers. Civilians were Tories displaced from areas no longer under British control. At least thirty-eight pieces of property in Newtown were designated

"Derelict Property assigned to Refugees." Here the British placed 155 women and children.[17]

More troublesome was the army. Joseph Tiedemann estimates
that as many as 8,192 British, German or provincial troops were
stationed on Long Island. Newtown became home at various
times for the Thirty-seventh, Thirty-eighth, and Fifty-fourth
Regiments, the Forty-second Grenadiers, Dee Corps, and
General Donop's Hessians. A return for the week of December
12, 1779, lists 2,556 men, 222 women, and 192 children provi-
sioned there—roughly twice as many as the entire population
of the town eight years earlier.[18]

Most of the troops settled into tents or huts erected in
Newtown's fields and meadows. Officers and prisoners of war
often stayed in people's homes. Generals James Robertson and
Sir Henry Clinton spent time at William Lawrence's and
Nathaniel Moore's. The American prisoner, Captain Raymond,
stayed at Dow Van Dyne's.[19]

The large number of troops and refugees in New York would
tax local resources—as an effect of official policy but also
because of criminal acts. The few existing Newtown memoirs
vividly recall pilfering. James Hedenburgh told of buried casks
full of stolen merchandise and commented that the crime was
not theft but getting caught. Aaron Furman remembered the
theft of a heifer and pigs; Elizabeth Brinkerhoff the stealing
of cabbages. The New York City newspapers also reported thefts
and rewards for stolen goods. On October 19, 1778 six people
broke into Joseph Hallett's house and stole ten guineas in a
green purse, and two watches, one gold and one silver. In April
of 1783 George Hunter offered a fifty-guinea reward for anyone
apprehending those who broke into the house of Jacob Ben-
net. County residents regularly reported horses missing.[20]

The British army and New York City's need for food, fuel and
transport resulted in the requisition of property, much of it lost
as army officers and paymasters pocketed the monies allocated
to pay for it. These losses fell on Whigs and Tories alike. Among
the loyalist claims are bills for horses, oxen, hay, oats, labor and
wood. Dow Ditmars noted 195 timber trees valued at £195 cut
by the engineers, and Richard Alsop claimed twenty-one
chestnut trees. When Casper Springsteen, a loyalist, refused to
lend his team of horses to the British, all of his fences were strip-
ped. Prices also rose. A cord of wood which cost 20 shillings

before the war cost thirty-five shillings in the winter of 1777–
1778. During the winter of 1780–1781 Queens supplied 10,500
cords of wood to New York City, and in the following July
another 4,500. Countymen also provided wood for soldiers
quartered in the county. After the war few stands of any size
would remain.[21]

The British occupation made changes in Newtown's economy
and also in the residents' perceptions of themselves. Pre-war
Newtown had been a quiet and safe place. That sense of safety
was shaken by the occupation. Between 1722, the first year that
court records are available, and the Revolution, only three
townsmen were prosecuted for assault. There were no murders
and apparently few thefts. During the war, violence, principal-
ly on the part of soldiers, became a part of life, known about
if not experienced. Farmers took the law into their own hands
and there it stayed. Mr. Woodward killed a soldier who was stealing his chickens and Mr. Cumberson killed another who was
breaking into his house. Mr. Rapelje wounded one soldier stealing a cow; his black slave killed the other. Yet, only William Furman appeared before a military court and he was charged with
abetting desertion, not assault or murder. Found guilty, he was
fined £40.[22]

Townsmen suffered not only from the army but also from the
depredations of refugees and of "whaleboatmen," pillagers who
raided the coast of northern Long Island from bases on the Connecticut mainland. While loss of property alienated townsmen
from the British, their chief long-term dissatisfaction was with
their vulnerability. Most were convinced by the end of the war
that they were unprotected. The British seemed powerless to
stop the depredations.[23]

Justice as a whole operated differently during the occupation. Before the war, petty cases came before justices of the
peace while more important civil and criminal infractions appeared before the court of common pleas or quarter sessions.
The court of common pleas continued to hear cases until 1779
but civilians could not sue soldiers. More importantly, military
needs for supplies and the problems that these raised were
decided by the military. In 1780 General James Robertson
replaced the court of common pleas with a court of police.
Justices also lost their power to hear petty cases. Queens County
inhabitants increasingly complained that justice under these
conditions was impossible.[24]

The net result of the occupation and martial law was a decline in townsmen's personal liberties. The sanctity of property, colonial Englishmen's most treasured right, fell before the needs of the military. Private homes were at the disposal of the army. Superintendent of the Court of Police George Duncan Ludlow, a Queens resident before the war, told farmers when to harvest. Even the right to come and go as one pleased was impaired by the military as they tried to control illicit trade with the rebelling Americans.[25]

Local government continued, even under martial law, but the flight of some Whigs such as Jacob Blackwell and Benjamin Coe, and the deaths of at least two town leaders in 1776 and 1777, resulted in new men holding town office between 1776 and 1783. Five men held seven or more terms of office from 1776 through October 1783. In each case, none of these men had been major town office holders before the war. Indeed, two of the five had never been elected to office before and only one had been a justice of the peace. These men did however share some characteristics. First, four of the five were Anglicans and the fifth was Dutch Reformed. All were officials in their churches. This supports Joseph Tiedemann's suggestion that in Newtown religion was the issue that divided men into Whigs and Tories. Second, each of these men would stand within the top 15 percent of the 1784 tax list. For the first time in its history Newtown selected town leaders from the top of the economic elite. Finally, all of the new leaders had identified themselves as loyal even before the British occupation by signing the letter to Rivington's *Gazette* disavowing the Continental Congress. These men were almost stereotypical loyalists. By electing them to office Newtown's voters were clearly telling the British that they were not a hostile community.[26]

Perhaps reflective of the significance of religion in dividing Whigs and Tories, the occupation allowed religious prejudices to emerge. In one of the first acts of vandalism following the Battle of Long Island, town Tories sawed off the steeple of the Presbyterian Church. The British later removed the pews and used the buildings as a prison. Finally, the structure was completely dismantled and the wood used for soldiers' huts. After the peace, town Presbyterians held services in the Dutch Reformed Church but during the war no services were held at all in Newtown and Presbyterians attended church in Jamaica.[27]

And yet, just as there were changes, there were also continuities, at least in form. Most townsmen remained in Newtown. If at most 16 percent of the adult males had left, at least 84 percent had stayed. The 1771 census named 189 householders (173 men and 16 women); lists of patriots and Tories from 1775 give some 151 men taking a stand. In 1779, during the height of the occupation, 93 townsmen sent a letter to Lieutenant Colonel Sterling of the Forty-second Regiment, thanking him and his officers for their "equitable, polite and friendly conduct during their winter stay among them." Of these 93 townsmen, 50 were on one of the earlier lists and an additional 31 either have Newtown surnames or appear in James Riker's *Annals of Newtown*. There are only eleven who might be new men.[28]

Apparently, most people stayed put and tried to conduct a normal life. The annual town meeting, held each April, elected officers as it had before the war. It also made petty rulings relating to such matters as the height of fences and permission to hang swinging gates. On April 14, 1778, townsmen held a special town meeting to decide whether Mr. Van Dyke could lease the town lands at the English Kills for a year. Town meeting minutes had long ceased to record anything other than elections and local regulations by 1776. The official record simply does not indicate that the town was occupied.[29]

The county also tried to function as it had before the war. Each year the county's elected board of supervisors, one from each town, met in October to apportion county expenses. In 1775, before the war, monies came from fines levied on Quakers during the Seven Years' War and from the liquor excise. The normal levy of taxes on each town, based on its yearly assessment was suspended, however. After expenses the county was left with £93-10-10 which it gave to the officers of the poor in Hempstead, Oyster Bay and the parish of Jamaica, which included Newtown.[30]

There are no county minutes for 1776, but the 1777 record looks much like 1775. Valentine Peters, treasurer since 1756, produced receipts for £58 of excise monies and bills worth £38 14s. Throughout the war the county would levy no taxes on its inhabitants. All revenues came from the liquor excise which covered the few costs of the county. Surplus revenue went to the county's three poor districts.[31]

Life also went on in other ways. Jamaica held a lottery to raise £780 for an Anglican glebe. Thomas Lambert Moore of Newtown advertised a school "to perfect a few young gentlemen (in addition to those already with him) in English, Greek and Latin. They can board in good families on easy terms." Joseph Burroughs advertised for a regular schoolmaster, a "single man, capable of instructing about twenty children in reading, writing and arithmetic." Peter Fitzsimmons opened a tavern at the house of widow Betts at Hallet's Cove Ferry while Peter Berton tried to sell his farm at the Queens Head tavern at Newtown Landing.[32]

Finally, something must be said about slaves living in Newtown during the British occupation. The rhetoric surrounding the decision to declare independence suggested that freedom, not slavery, was the natural state of humankind. Slaves must have heard at least some discussion of tyranny and freedom. Moreover, the disorder marking the beginning of the Revolution and the occupation presented opportunities for escape. Some slaves did attempt to leave. In 1779 "Jeff," a slave belonging to Bernardus Bloom, carried a $5.00 reward. The same year, Charles, "a negro of yellowish cast, and plays on the fiddle," left Casper Springsteen. Three years later, Adam, wearing an officer's old red coat faced with white and a gold basket button, and Nero, "a likely young Guinea negro fellow . . . who had on a blue frieze shooting jacket . . . and an old flapped hat both escaped from their masters." In 1779, John Deacon offered a one guinea reward for Isabella, a mulatto girl "who ran away from Jacobus Lint . . . in man's clothes." An advertisement four years later was even more descriptive. "Run away, Kate, born in the family of Jacob Bennet, wears her hair very high and straight up, over a roll, with a great deal of pomatum; a great talker; took a calico short-gown, with figures of horses, carriages and soldiers in blue and yellow colors, particularly a row of soldiers round the bottom of it, and several caps with long ears." A five-dollar reward was offered.[33]

And yet these cases are few. Only three more Newtown runaways were advertised in the newspapers. Just as most whites stayed put, so did most blacks. Runaway ads had dotted the newspapers throughout the colonial period and while they may have increased somewhat, they in no way suggest a major redistribution of the black population. Newtown would enter the newly independent state of New York with most of its slave force intact.[34]

The British defeat and subsequent evacuation produced additional changes in Newtown. Just as it is difficult to estimate how many Whigs left Newtown after the American defeat in 1776, it is hard to know how many British sympathizers left Newtown when the British withdrew. Joseph Tiedemann estimates that 5 to 6 percent of Queens County's prewar population became refugees. Various records suggest that twenty-two Newtowners, there by 1775, became active Tories. Of these, thirteen may have left the town in 1784. The rest either died before the war ended, stayed put, or disappeared from the record. Again assuming, as was done for the Whigs, that there were 225 adult males in Newtown in 1775, then 6 percent left, a number consistent with Tiedemann's estimate. Of the thirteen exiles, seven can be traced to either Nova Scotia or New Brunswick. None of the Newtown exiles can be tracked to Great Britain.[35]

Not only did Tories leave at this time, but exiled Whigs such as Gabriel Furman, Abraham Furman, Abraham Riker and John Berrien Riker returned. These men were exempted from the 1784 tax list, the primary source for Newtown's immediate postwar population and it is difficult to determine how many came back. Some, such as Jacob Blackwell, died there in 1780. Captain Richard Lawrence, a prisoner-of-war, returned to Newtown to die in 1781. Abraham Riker died at Valley Forge in 1778.[36] Others undoubtedly stayed in Orange County or in New Jersey, where they had found refuge.

The relatively small number of Whig and Loyalist exiles obscures the overall dynamic nature of Newtown's population from 1771 to 1800. Much of this change was natural. Of the 189 names which appeared on the 1771 census, only 87 appear on a 1784 tax list. Since this list excluded the Whig exiles it is not a complete record of taxpayers, and of course it also exempted those persons too poor to be taxed. Even with these deficiencies, however, a comparison of the two lists is useful. As many as 55 of the 102 residents absent from the 1784 list may have died and another 8 were known Whig exiles or departed Loyalists. This leaves 39 men who may have left Newtown.[37]

The 1784 tax list contains the names of 175 male residents, 110 of which are absent from the 1771 census. Of these 110

names, only 21 cannot be identified in community records
before the Revolution. Moreover, of these twenty-one, only fourteen cannot be found intermarrying in Newtown's established
families. The 1784 lists therefore suggests that few new men
had settled in the town during these years. The lack of dupli-
cation among names on the two lists is more the result of householders dying and sons coming of age.[38]

The 1771 census lists sixteen female heads of households of
whom fourteen are identified as widows. By 1784 the number
of females taxed as owners of property had increased to thirty.
At least fourteen were widows. Comparison of the two lists for
remarriage rates or persistence is impossible since the 1771 census omits women's first names, referring to them only as Widow
Furman, or Widow Rapelje. Phoebe Coe appears on both lists.
The larger number of women on the tax list also reflects changes
of property-holding, at least temporarily. Anna Van Dyne was
taxed for properties worth £650, but some of these had belonged to Dow Van Dyne, her exiled husband. These holdings probably represented a dower right, which now reverted to her
while his remaining properties were confiscated by the state.[39]

The 1790 federal census shows that Newtown's population
consisted of 2,111 souls living in 293 households. Of these 2,111
people, 1,526 were white, 533 were slaves, and 52 were free
blacks. The listing of household heads in 1790 shows the impact of population movement and mortality in Newtown. The
293 households were headed by 243 white males, 24 white
females, 23 free black males and 3 free black females. There
are 131 surnames on the list of which 37, or 28 percent, appear
for the first time.

A full 72 percent of families had been in Newtown since at
least 1784; some of them, like the Coes and the Moores, since
1664. Eighteen of the new names disappeared from subsequent
censuses; but nineteen remained at least until the 1800 census. Of the ninety-five surnames which had appeared before
1790, eleven were gone by 1800. Perhaps not too surprisingly,
these represent only thirteen households. Those most apt to
leave seem to have been newcomers or those without apparent
extended kinship ties to Newtown.[40]

Of the 243 male household heads in Newtown in 1790, 149,
or 61 percent, had been there as of 1784; 135 would be there

in 1800. Between the two censuses some 67 may have died. This means that of the 243 male heads of household living in Newtown in 1790, only 40, or 16 percent, would have moved. Because of limited economic opportunity, their now-dependent sons would undoubtedly have a higher mobility rate.[41]

Twenty-four white women headed households in 1790. Only Phoebe Coe was listed in 1784 but widows of deceased patriots would have been exempted from taxpaying and not on the list. Nine were still listed as female heads of households in 1800. The evidence is too scanty to show if the fifteen women who disappear from the record remarried, migrated or died.

Black heads of household are first listed in 1790. Of the twenty-three males, only two, Portland and Jacob Solomon, appear in 1800. None of the women do. Perhaps the blacks left. They might have become laborers in the homes of others since the 1800 census shows that at least forty-one of Newtown's ninety-four free persons were listed under white household heads.[42]

The 1800 census shows 2,224 people of whom 1,618 were white, 512 slave, and 94 free black. These numbers represent an increase in total population of 113, for an annual growth rate of .53 percent. This is a much lower rate of growth than for New York State as a whole with its annual rate of 7.32 percent. The 1810 census shows that this growth rate increased slightly as population increased by 213 for an annual growth rate of .95 percent a year.[43]

Newtown's 326 households in 1800 were headed by 288 white males, 25 white females, 9 black males, 2 black females and two other unidentifiable free blacks. These households were divided into154 white surnames. Of these 57 family names, 37 percent were new and 63 percent remained from 1790. Of the 57 family names 41 would be gone by 1810. As was the case previously, those leaving were more likely to have come as single households rather than as small clusters of families. Of those departing, 34, or 83 percent, were single households.[44]

The census records allow us to see—roughly for 1790, more clearly for 1800—the age, sex and racial composition of the population. Among the whites in 1790, there were 420 males sixteen years old and over and 353 males under sixteen. Fully 46 percent of the town's males were children. There were 753 white females in town giving Newtown whites a sex ratio of 1.03. In 1790 it was the only town in Queens County with more white males than females.[45]

The 1800 and 1810 censuses allow for finer gender and age discriminations. Table 1 presents gender ratios by age in 1800 and 1810. Table 2 presents a breakdown of the white population in terms of age and gender. Since the ratio of males to females at birth is just about 1.00, and since the overall gender ratio for the town in 1800 is .995 and in 1810 is .99, there are clearly outside factors skewing Newtown's gender ratio for those between the ages of sixteen and twenty-six. The excess females in the 26-to-45 age range in 1810 is a continuation of the very low gender ratio of those in the 16-to-26 age range ten years earlier. Both censuses show a return to something closer to the norm for the oldest population group.[46]

The notable gender ratio anomalies lie in the 16 to 26 age group of the 1800 census and the 16-to-45 age group of the 1810 census. The lack of males in the 1800 16-26 age group probably reflects the lack of opportunity in Newtown for younger sons. Like so many long-settled towns, Newtown had no free lands to distribute. Moreover, the pre-Revolutionary land conveyances show that large tracts of land rarely reached the market after the mid-1700s, and when they did they were expensive. Western Long Island later turned to garden farming for the New York City market and light industry, such as fulling, tanning and hat making, but these economic adaptations came after 1800.[47]

The limited economic opportunity which drove out young men also discouraged new families from remaining in town. This does not mean that townsmen were impoverished, but it does point to at least the perception of an economy more closed than elsewhere. New York's population was growing rapidly in New York City and in upstate areas. This high rate of growth exceeded that of Queens County.

Newtown's low growth rate was primarily a result of emigration, rather than low fertility or high mortality. As in 1790, a large number of the town's inhabitants were minors (See Table 2). In 1800, 48 percent of the white population was under sixteen; in 1810, 45 percent was under sixteen, rates characteristic of a "young" population. Of the white population in 1800, 17 percent was forty-five or older; 18 percent of the 1810 population was in that age group. These percentages suggest

TABLE 1
WHITE GENDER RATIO BY AGE: 1800 AND 1810

	1800	1810
Under 10	.96	1.09
10 to 16	1.16	1.10
16 to 26	.74	.85
26 to 45	1.02	.83
Over 45	1.14	1.07

Sources: "Schedule of the Whole Number of Persons Contained within the County of Queens. Township of Newtown [1800]"; "County of Queens. Population Schedules of the Third Census of the United States, 1810."

TABLE 2
WHITE POPULATION BY AGE AND GENDER: 1800 AND 1810

Population in 1800

Age	Male		Female		Total		
	No.	%	No.	%	No.	%	Cum. %
Under 10	253	31	263	32	516	31.9	31.9
10 to 16	136	17	118	14	254	15.7	47.6
16 to 26	98	12	132	16	230	14.2	61.8
26 to 45	174	22	170	21	344	21.3	83.1
Over 45	146	18	128	16	274	16.9	100.0
Total	807	100	811	99	1618	100	100

Source: "Schedule of the Whole Number of Persons Contained within the County of Queens. Township of Newtown [1800]."

Population in 1810

Age	Male		Female		Total		
	No.	%	No.	%	No.	%	Cum. %
Under 10	263	28	241	26	504	27.0	27.0
10 to 16	172	19	156	16	328	17.6	44.6
16 to 26	164	18	193	21	357	19.1	63.7
26 to 45	152	16	183	20	335	18.0	81.7
Over 45	178	19	165	18	343	18.3	100.0
Total	929	100	938	101	1867	100	100

Source: "County of Queens. Population Schedules of the Third Census of the United States, 1810."

a fairly low death rate. This population configuration suggests a moderate birth rate, a low death rate, and something else—emigration or war—to account for the lower percentages in the middle.[48]

Age and gender ratios can provide a sense of what a town's population looked like and suggest ongoing demographic and economic processes. However, censuses also show household sizes and composition. Newtown's white population clearly lived in household groups, not as solitary individuals. In 1790, 71 percent of the 243 white male households contained between four and eight white members. Only three white males lived alone: Philip Edsall, Sr., was seventy-seven years old with grown children; Samuel Lawrence was a widower in his fifties whose children had already died; Jacob Rapalje seems also to have been in his fifties but there is no further information about him. Fifteen males lived in a household of ten or more. By 1800, households were smaller. Fifty-three percent of the 288 white households with male heads contained four to eight free people. Twenty-seven percent held three or fewer. Men still lived with others, however, as only seven men of 288, or 2 percent, lived alone. Twenty-two households, or 8 percent held ten or more free people. The decline in the size of households is undoubtedly related to the exodus of young dependent males and the concomitant aging of the remaining population.[49]

White female heads of households lived in much smaller units. Of the twenty-four female-headed households in 1790, 71 percent were units of four or less. No white woman lived alone although fourteen lived with other females. Two women shared a household with males under sixteen. By 1800 Newtown's twenty-five female-headed households also showed a slight trend toward becoming smaller. A full 80 percent contained four or fewer free persons. One woman lived alone.

The experience of Newtown's free blacks was much different. A small population to begin with, free blacks lived singly or in small groups in 1790. Fourteen of the twenty-three male household heads of 1790 lived alone. Perhaps their families were still slaves living in the households of their masters. Another seven lived with one or two other people. Of the three women, one lived alone and the other two lived in households of four people, probably children. The census suggests that some of the men lived relatively close to one another, but the life of a single householder is qualitatively different from the life of one who lives with others. One senses that free blacks lived a lonelier life, especially given a cultural norm that stressed living with others.

By 1800, although there were more free blacks, there were fewer free black household heads. Nine men and two women are listed by name; two entries of household heads are illegible. Only two men lived alone; the others lived in households of up to seven people. One woman lived with one person, the other with four. The economic conditions which made it difficult for younger sons to stay in Newtown must also have worked against free blacks. Some left; others became dependents in white households.

Newtown's slave population lived more with other blacks than Newtown's freedmen. In 1790, the town's 533 slaves were divided among 141 slave owners. Forty-one of these owned one slave, which meant that the remaining 492 slaves, about 92 percent of the total slave population, lived in households with at least one other black, and in many cases several blacks. Simon Remsen owned thirteen slaves and both William Sackett and Jacob Miller owned eleven. Eighty percent of Newtown's slaves lived in households with four or more slaves. For them, life must have been less isolated than for Newtown's free blacks.

In 1800 the town had somewhere between 508 and 512 slaves, a decline of 21 or about 4 percent of the slave population.[50] However, some manumitting had already begun by then. Even before the 1799 law which gradually freed all of New York State's slaves, John Mercier, Mrs. Deborah Smith, and Anthony and Benjamin Betts had freed their bondspeople.[51] One hundred and thirty-nine households continued to hold slaves, a decline of two from 1790. Distribution of slaves also remained about the same. Forty-four slaves or 9 percent lived in single slave households. Only William Sackett owned twelve slaves and Thomas Lawrence owned ten. Seventy-five percent of the slave population lived in households of four or more slaves. The only real difference for Newtown's bondsmen was that now a number of them lived in households that also included free blacks. For both groups this probably meant a richer social environment.

As before the Revolution and during the conflict, some slaves tried to escape bondage. In 1794 both Pompey and Joe ran away

from their masters. Pompey was about thirty, tall, dark with
a limp and "a down look." Joe was about twenty, about five
foot four inches, and "has the third finger of one of his hands
broken, and is considerable larger than his other fingers."
Rewards were offered for both.[52]

By 1790, Newtown's slaveholding was unusual, even for
Queens County. In both 1790 and 1800, Newtown had more
slaves than any other county town. In 1800, only Jamaica had
fewer free blacks. Looked at another way, in 1790, a full 25 percent of the town's population were bondspeople. In 1800, this
number had dropped but slightly, to 23 percent. While it is hard
to know exactly what slaves did in Newtown, they were probably agricultural and domestic laborers. This large force would
have made it even more difficult for free white labor to compete and would have been yet another factor leading to the exodus of Newtown's males in the 16-to-26 age group.

The Revolution made some temporary differences in
Newtown's demographic history, but the census figures suggest
that other processes, ongoing before the war and continuing
after it, were more important. This seems to be true also for
both Newtown's economy and local politics. The demands of
the British army for firewood decimated Newtown's woodlands.
Livestock and farm equipment such as carts also were destroyed
or taken. The evidence suggests, however, that while individuals
must have suffered, the overall economy of the town sprang
back rather quickly. County supervisors rated Newtown at
£3,166 in 1769, £3,565 in 1775, £4,507 in 1784 and £3,063 in
1786. The tax list of 1784, even though it excludes exiled Whigs,
suggests some prosperity and also accords with the pattern of
wealth distribution seen elsewhere in the countryside. Newtown's total taxable property was worth £109,691, a figure
which excluded bonds, notes and mortgages. The poorest 30 percent of the tax list controlled 2.5 percent of the taxable wealth;
the upper 10 percent controlled 37 percent.[53]

Another measure of Newtown's relative standing can be seen
in the numbers of men holding enough property to vote. New
York's constitution of 1777 gave all adult males who possessed
a £20 freehold or paid rents of 40 shillings the right to vote
for assemblymen and all those who held a £100 freehold, free
of debt, the right to elect senators and the governor in addi-

tion to assemblymen. In the 1795 census, taken to count the number of state electors, Newtown had 77 men who qualified to elect only assemblymen and another 199 who qualified to elect senators for a total electorate of 276 men. Both the 1790 and the 1800 censuses allow estimates of the total population of white males twenty-one and older, thereby showing what percentage of townsmen held at least enough wealth to vote. Since the 1790 census shows 353 males over sixteen, which should indicate that 282 men were over twenty-one, 98 percent of Newtown's males could vote for the lower house; 71 percent could vote in all elections. Those with the lower qualifications may have been younger men, sons waiting to inherit, since 63 of the 77 were tenants.[54]

In 1808, 74 men held the lower freehold and another 240 held the higher for a total voting population of 314. The 1800 census shows 369 men over twenty-one, 85 percent of whom could have voted for the lower house and 65 percent in all elections. Newtown's percentage of eligible voters had dropped, suggesting that economic conditions had deteriorated since 1790. Even so, a solid majority of adult males could at least vote for the state's lower house and for United States congressmen.[55]

Newtown's economy was still mainly agricultural. An 1810 census of arts and manufactures shows that Queens County as a whole was yet to invest in manufacturing. There was some small scale cloth production—7 carding machines, 8 fulling mills, one cotton manufactory, 486 looms and 40 spindles. In contrast, Dutchess County had 25 carding machines, 35 fulling mills, 5 cotton manufactories, 1,342 looms and 2,978 spindles. Queens had no iron, sugar, glass, tobacco, chocolate or gunpowder manufacturing. It did make hats and paper, tanned hides and distilled a mere 2,000 gallons of alcohol. Dutchess County distillers, on the other hand, produced ten times as much and New York City a prodigious 377,298 gallons.[56]

Advertisements for town properties also continued to stress agricultural products, with emphasis on orchards and cider, and to emphasize Newtown's proximity to New York City. In 1787 Samuel Furman advertised a farm near Newtown Landing containing 100 acres of land, "of which 40 are excellent meadow, 9 of woodland, and the rest of good arable ground." The property also contained two dwelling houses, barn, stables, and a "never failing spring." Eight years later, the farm of Abraham

Polhemus was offered. It comprised three acres of woodland, sixty to seventy acres of arable meadow, a four-room house, out-buildings including a wagon house with granary above, cider mill, mill house and weaving shop. The property also included a young orchard containing 300 apple trees, grafted trees, pears and other fruits. In 1794 it had produced 40 barrels of cider and 150 barrels of Newtown pippins. In 1796, Peter Alburtis offered a 170-acre farm, "about seven miles from Brooklyn ferry, by land, and six by water," which contained thirty-five acres of woods, "young thrifty timber," and salt meadow. The large house contained three stories with eight rooms, a garret and two unfinished chambers. Two orchards containing 500 apple trees—as well as pears, peaches, plums and English cher-ries—helped supply the cider mill.[57]

Each of the three properties listed for sale was beyond the reach of Newtown's younger sons or the poor. The census mater-ials show that a fair percentage of those voting for assembly-men rented their lands. Those with potential earning power but without prospects left for other parts. The poor remained to become the responsibility of the town. The war undoubtedly worked against some. At least a few townsmen never return-ed, leaving widows and orphans behind. During the war, the county supervisors had remanded excess funds to Jamaica Parish. After the war, with the disestablishment of the Church of England, the poor became the town's sole responsibility and town budgets quickly reflected an increase in the amount spent. Whereas Jamaica Parish, which included Jamaica, Newtown and Flushing, had received £23 in 1777 and £25 in 1778, in 1784, when the method of accounting changed, the county as-sessed the town £70 for the poor. That year the town also elected its first poor masters. Ensuing years would see the levy for the poor rise. In 1790 the town raised £80, in 1791 £130, in 1793 £170, in 1795 £200, and in 1798 £250. Unfortunately, the records omit the names and number of those receiving aid.[58]

Poor relief in Newtown apparently took the form of home relief or boarding out. In 1796 the town meeting appointed Ben-jamin Coe, David Titus, and William Sackett to "inquire into the most eligible way of supporting the poor of this town and what sum will be required to put the town house in sufficient order for that purpose." Their report apparently recommend-ed against this use of town property since in 1798 and then again in 1800 it was leased out. However, in looking into separate dwellings for the poor the town was following the lead of Hempstead. Robert Cray argues that this shift from home relief, which kept the poor integrated into the town, to a poorhouse, which segregated the poor, was a way of controlling both the poor and their keepers. He further suggests that it was symptomatic of a breakdown in rural values and cohesion. It is probably no coincidence that Hempstead was the largest county town and potentially the least manageable. Immediately after the war it would divide into two towns. Newtown, on the other hand, could still carry on as before.[59]

Poor relief furnished the town with a new responsibility, but otherwise formal town government did little more than it had before the Revolution. Townsmen continued to pass rules governing fence heights and the hobbling of horses, and they continued to rent out town properties. As in the past they defended town properties against others. When Henry Mott encroached upon the public landing, townsmen, at a special town meeting, voted to spend up to $1,000 defending their rights. Mott came to terms without a lawsuit.[60]

The most consistent concern of the town meeting was the election of town officials. The end of the war brought a change in town officers just as the beginning of the war had. During the period of the British occupation, townsmen had elected those acceptable to the British. With the British evacuation, townsmen initially elected persons who had been active patriots. Of the eight men who held more than eleven years of town office between the evacuation of Newtown and 1800, five had been active Whigs either immediately before the occupation or afterwards. Four had voted to support the Continental Congress in 1775. At least five had served in the militia with the rank of second lieutenant or higher on the eve of the Battle of Long Island. Three—Daniel Lawrence, Benjamin Coe and Samuel Riker—would hold state offices after 1777.

Newtown's new leadership had military and other political experience that was newly gained. They had not held many prewar town offices. Samuel Riker had been a highway overseer and assessor, Daniel Lawrence a highway overseer. In part, their previous lack of office-holding related to their ages. Samuel Riker was born in 1743, Daniel Lawrence in 1739. Two others for whom birth dates are available were born in 1741 and 1758. As a group, these men came of age politically in the years 1775-1783 when office in Newtown was unavailable to them.[61]

The return of civilian government was more apparent in the courts than in the town meeting. While the courts opened in 1784, the records for Queens County are incomplete, and civil cases against county loyalists were also filed in Dutchess County, where many of the exiled Whigs lived. In July 1784, William Sackett sued Justice Richard Alsop, Abraham Polhemus, Jr. and Sr., and Charles and George Debevoice "for trespass in cutting of his woodland from November 16, 1779 to March 1780, for the construction of huts, and for fuel for the use of the thirty-seventh and fifty-fourth Regiments of British troops and the Regiment de Landgrave, to his damage £800." The defendants argued that Long Island was then under military rule and that they were under orders from Governor Tryon "to take wood from the most convenient places, giving rebel woods the preference." William Sackett won this case but was only awarded £190 damages and 6d in costs, far less than the losses claimed.[62]

What is striking is the lack of wholesale litigation by neighbor against neighbor. In July 1783 Jacob and John Moore, Lieutenant James Marr and Captain Dow Van Dyne were indicted in Albany and Dutchess Counties for adhering to the cause of the enemy and told to appear before the supreme court to show why their properties should not be forfeited.[75] Only Dow Van Dyne lost his lands although other collaborators might have seen the problems coming and sold while they could. Van Dyne later claimed 290 acres valued at £1,671 sterling for which the British awarded him £900. New York State sold his farm to Thomas McFarren, a New York City speculator in confiscated lands, for £1,900, New York currency.[63]

This is not to say that individuals quickly forgot or in their hearts forgave. James Riker, who as a young man growing up in Newtown knew survivors of the Revolution, noted that "The social and domestic circles of Newtown felt for years the blighting influences of these deep-seated feuds; indeed the alienations thus cherished only terminated in many instances at the grave, and died as the generation itself passed away." But overall, there was little overt hostility. Henry Onderdonk, Jr., attributed the few successful suits to "Able lawyers, disagreeing jurors, *certioraris* and the law's delay." More recent scholarship suggests other patterns.[64]

Edward Countryman, looking at the rhythms of anti-loyalist legislation in the New York State Assembly has identified three phases: The Conservative Retreat, 1777–1782, The Radical Ascendancy, 1781–1786, and the Rise of Conservative Nationalism, 1784–1788. The Trespassing Act under which William Sackett sued was passed during the radical phase of the New York State Assembly. Countryman concludes that conservative forces eventually won control of the Assembly and these had a vested interest in creating a neutral climate for loyalists who had often been their friends and who shared their less democratic, pro-commercial interests.[65]

Joseph Tiedemann, focusing on the British occupation, provides a more sociological explanation: British exploitation had blurred the line between closet patriots, neutrals, and Tories. All had suffered together and experienced British corruption, contempt and incompetence. By the war's end the British had thoroughly alienated everyone. Townsmen became, in Tiedemann's words, "patriots by default." Perhaps as important, large numbers of former loyalists remained in Queens. Incorporating them into the ongoing life of the county allowed for a speedier return to ordinary life and insured acceptance of the Revolution. Even former exiles felt it was safe to return, as did "Thirty Loyalists (among them Mr. Moore, of Newtown.)"[66]

The Revolution affected individuals, but the long-term effects of the war on Newtown and even places like New York City seem far slighter than might be expected. Part of the reason for the relative ease with which civilians reestablished life was the nature of eighteenth-century warfare. British commanders at least tried to spare civilians and their property. After the earliest battles, lower New York saw little formal combat; scorched earth policies and the implementation of "total war" still lay in the future. And the occupation left at least some of the political infrastructure intact. Towns and counties still functioned minimally. In addition, townsmen's expectations were limited. This was especially true politically. Under George III, New Yorkers preferred that government which governed least and least expensively. Assemblymen passed local regulatory statutes without much fuss but balked at most projects requiring taxation. Newtowners' voting behavior suggests that this attitude persisted.[67]

The political integration of the town into New York State may be analyzed by considering the town's choice of candidates and the exercise of the franchise. What these choices actually meant to townsmen is more speculative, since the thinking, hopes, and aspirations that informed their behavior is for the most part hidden behind a lack of evidence. Before 1784, Queens County inhabitants could not vote for Assemblymen. They were represented, however, by what were called "ordinance members" —exiled countymen chosen initially by those who wrote the state constitution. Philip Edsall, Daniel Lawrence, Benjamin Coe and Benjamin Birdsall sat for Queens from 1777 to 1783. Three of the four were from Newtown; Benjamin Birdsall was from Oyster Bay. Never before or since would Newtown have so many townsmen in any state representative body. Only Benjamin Coe would be reelected when the voters of Queens County could again choose for themselves.[68]

Although complete voting returns by town are lost, enough survive to give some idea of whom townsmen chose. The town vote for various candidates still exist for the 1788 Assembly election and the Poughkeepsie ratifying convention, the 1789, 1792, 1795, and 1798 gubernatorial elections, the 1792, 1794, 1795, and 1798 state senate elections and the 1793 and 1795 congressional elections.[69]

Table 3 summarizes Newtown's election results. The data suggest that townsmen approved of the United States Constitution but also supported Governor George Clinton, an Antifederalist and eventual Republican. Two patterns emerge from Newtown's choice of candidates. The first is that Newtown often backed losing candidates. This outcome is especially clear in the state senate races where Newtown was part of the "Southern District," a large and populous area which included New York City and Kings, Queens, Richmond, Suffolk, and Westchester Counties. The town's or even the county's voice was swallowed up by the larger voting populations in other parts of the district. The second pattern which emerges is that the town usually supported Thomas Jefferson's Republicans.

Newtown's choices of Nathaniel Seaman, Francis Lewis, Prior Townsend and Whitehead Cornell for the 1788 General Assembly did poorly in the county. Of the seven candidates, Newtown's four came in last with only Whitehead Cornell elected. The three defeated candidates were all Federalists; Whitehead Cornell was an Antifederalist. If these divisions helped voters decide on assemblymen in 1788 then Newtown must be labelled a Federalist stronghold. This preference would be clearer three days later when the election for delegates to the ratifying convention took place.[70]

Election of delegates to the ratifying convention came at the end of an energetic campaign to sway votes. However, as Robert Ernst has recently pointed out, ''Precisely what Long Islanders thought of that document as formulated by the Philadelphia Convention of 1787 can hardly be determined.''[71] Town minutes are silent about the Constitution and there are as yet no Queens

TABLE 3

ELECTION RESULTS FROM NEWTOWN: 1788-1798

Election	Newtown's Choice	Party[a]	Election Result
1788 State Assembly	Nathaniel Seaman	F	Lost
	Francis Lewis, Jr.	F	Lost
	Prior Townsend	F	Lost
	Whitehead Cornell	A	Won
1788 Ratifying Convention	Isaac Ledyard	F	Lost
	Francis Lewis, Jr.	F	Lost
	Hendrick Onderdonk	F	Lost
	Prior Townsend	F	Lost
1789 Gubernatorial	George Clinton	A	Won
1792 Gubernatorial	George Clinton	A	Won
1795 Gubernatorial	Robert Yates	R	Lost
1798 Gubernatorial	Robert R. Livingston	R	Lost
1792 Senate	Francis Lewis, Jr.	F	Lost
	John Schenck	A	Won
1794 Senate	David Gelston	R	Lost
	Unclear[b]	?	?
1795 Senate	David Gelston	R	Lost
	Benjamin Coe	R	Lost
1798 Senate	DeWitt Clinton	R	Won
	John Schenck	R	Won
1793 U.S. Congress	Thomas Tredwell	R	Won
1795 U.S. Congress	Samuel Jones	F	Lost

Sources: See text for citations.

a. F=Federalist; A=Antifederalist; R=Republican.

b. The name and vote tally is illegible in *Greenleaf's New York Journal & Patriotic Register*. Newtown's second choice can therefore not be determined.

County newspapers. However, eight candidates ran for the four county positions—four Federalists and four Antifederalists. The county elected four Antifederalists, but the vote was actually split. Newtown, Flushing and Jamaica, the westernmost towns, gave their votes to the Federalist candidates. They chose Dr. Isaac Ledyard, Francis Lewis, Jr., Hendrick Onderdonk and Prior Townsend. Their four choices all lost, overwhelmed by the 706 votes of North Hempstead and the 999 of South Hempstead.[72]

It is difficult to know why western Long Island and Newtown in particular voted Federalist, especially since Newtown would turn against the Federalist party later. These areas had suffered more under the occupation than other towns and perhaps wished for more order because of that. Also, they were home to former loyalists who would favor creating a strong central government. It is also possible that men tended to vote for those they knew. Dr. Isaac Ledyard, a political friend of Alexander Hamilton, had moved to Newtown after the Revolution buying the one farm confiscated from a loyalist. He appears in the 1790 and 1800 censuses; an Ann Ledyard is listed in 1810. He held no town office by 1788 but in 1789 signed a letter to *The Daily Advertiser* as an elector or inhabitant of Queens County endorsing the Hamiltonian slate for governor and lieutenant governor.[73]

Francis Lewis, Jr., was the son of the signer of the Declaration of Independence, Francis Lewis. He lived in Flushing, Newtown's neighbor to the east. Hendrick Onderdonk came from North Hempstead and Prior Townsend from Oyster Bay. Of the four winning Antifederalists, three came from the Hempsteads and one from Oyster Bay.[74]

Newtown's voters may have favored the Constitution in 1788 but they did not necessarily vote for the candidates whom Federalists supported for other office. Only one year later, Queens county elected George Clinton governor over Robert Yates by a vote of 482 to 124. Newtown chose Clinton by the overwhelming majority of 101 to 5. This massive support for Clinton took place in spite of Isaac Ledyard's public support of Yates. However, 1788 was still too early for the party formation which would take place in the 1790s. Townsmen apparently voted their interest as they saw it. This interest led them to favor the Constitution on the national level and the Clintonians on the state level. Three years later Clinton again won, this time defeating John Jay. All six towns gave their vote to Clinton. In the 1795 election for governor and lt. governor, the town voted solidly for Robert Yates and William Floyd. The Federalists John Jay and Stephen van Rensselaer won, swept in by the overwhelming majorities they acquired in South Hempstead. In 1798, John Jay ran for governor against Chancellor Robert R. Livingston. Jay polled only 36 of Newtown's 113 votes, but he won the county 507 to 317 with the help of South Hempstead's 214 to 41 victory. Newtown and Jamaica had voted Republican, the rest of the county Federalist.[75]

Townsmen seemed to have become Democratic Republicans. This preference clearly shows in the state senate elections. In 1792 Newtown voted for Francis Lewis, Jr., a Federalist, and John Schenck, an Antifederalist. Schenck, from Hempstead, supported a state university and consistently opposed Vermont's entering the Union. These positions would seem to make him an ally of George Clinton and thus probably a Republican. Lewis and Schenck were also the county's choices, but only Schenck was elected.[76]

In the 1794 election for state senator, Newtown supported David Gelston, a New York City merchant originally from Suffolk County. A close friend of George Clinton, he was the first president of the Democratic Society of New York City. Gelston came in last in the southern district; the Federalists Matthew Clarkson and Richard Hatfield took Queens County and won the election. The next year Gelston again ran, and he and Benjamin Coe, a townsman and Republican, won Newtown's vote. Gelston came in second in the county, but neither candidate took the district. In 1798 townsmen favored DeWitt Clinton, George Clinton's nephew and sometime resident of Newtown, and John Schenck. Both Clinton and Schenck won their offices.[77]

Townsmen also participated in national politics. In the congressional race of 1793 they supported Thomas Tredwell of Huntington, who was swept into office by the 1,069 votes of his native Suffolk County. Originally an Antifederalist, Tredwell was an ally of James Madison. Two years later, Newtowners voted for Samuel Jones, an Antifederalist delegate to the Poughkeepsie ratifying convention who later changed his mind and helped his fellow countymen ratify the Constitution. Jones has to be one of the more intriguing Queens County politicians. A Tory during the war, he was afterward a member of the ratifying convention. He was also a distinguished jurist, an Antifederalist who ratified the Constitution, a Clintonian but later a Federalist. He seems most of all to have been a pragmatist. Reportedly, when asked why he always ended up on the winning side, he replied, "When my troops won't follow me I follow them." In this case he failed to follow enough of them and lost the congressional election to Jonathan Nicoll Havens.[78]

Jonathan Nicoll Havens only received three of sixty-six votes that Newtowners cast in 1795, but he should have been their candidate. A "learned and conscientious Jeffersonian," Havens championed Newtown's small farmers.[79] His defeat suggests that townsmen reserved the right to judge some things for themselves. They knew Samuel Jones and apparently respected him. He was a countyman, which might have made some difference. In 1795, party lines were still supple enough that other factors could shape election results.

The Newtown of the 1790s was possibly more politically aware than colonial Newtown. Political activity took place on a number of different levels. First, there was active campaigning and organizing for office, as indicated by this 1793 announcement:

> At a respectable meeting of the electors of Newtown, at
> Abraham Rapalye's, February 27th [1793], Colonel Daniel
> Lawrence in the Chair, it was requested that a correspond-
> ence should be entered into with the other towns of this
> county to fix on a proper person to represent them in the le-
> gislature;
> *Resolved*, that Isaac Corsa, John Lawrence and Robert
> Moore, Esqrs., be a committee for that purpose;
> *Resolved*, That it is the intent of this meeting to support
> Samuel Riker for Ably.[80]

Riker was a townsman and apparently a Jeffersonian, On March 2nd a group of countymen met at a Jamaica tavern and nominated the Federalist Dr. Isaac Ledyard and John B. Hicks. In the actual election none of these three won.[81]

Townsmen also took part in partisan national affairs, just as they had participated in controversial activity in 1775. On December 26, 1798 "At a general and large meeting of the freeholders and inhabitants of Newtown," it was unanimously resolved "that the Alien and Sedition laws ought to be repealed," and a committee was appointed to ask the other county towns to address Congress. Among those making up the committee were Samuel Riker, and Benjamin Coe, members of Newtown's political elite. The committee soon found, as in 1775, that others were opposed to their measures. Newtown's meeting demonstrated party politics in action, since the Alien and Sedition Acts were specifically aimed at Jefferson's Democratic Republicans.[82]

Choosing candidates was one means of political expression open to Newtowners. The act of voting was another. In 1795, 276 townsmen could vote for state assemblymen and United States congressmen while 199 could vote for governor and state senator. The number of these potential electors who actually voted is hard to know since they could cast their ballots for a slate composed of mutiple candidates. Table 4 summarizes the number voting for each of the elections where information is available. In 1788, townsmen cast 303 votes for four assemblymen. If each elector cast a ballot for four men, then 76 men voted, for a turnout of roughly 28 percent, hardly a massive exercise of the franchise. Possibly this number is too low since some men probably did not vote for all four but for fewer candidates. However, the turnout for Queens County as a whole was apparently only 23 percent. Voters were not being galvanized by their sense of civic responsibility in this election.[83]

The election to Poughkeepsie's ratifying convention saw a larger turnout. Townmen cast a total of 435 votes for a possible electorate of 109 men or 40 percent. Given that every man over twenty-one could vote, regardless of property holdings, this has to be seen as a low turnout. Even so, Newtown's record was better than Queens County's 30 percent voter participation. As Linda Grant DePauw notes, "New Yorkers found many personal and public matters competing with the Constitution for their attention."[84]

Voter turnout increased after 1788. The gubernatorial elections show a fair amount of voter interest ranging from 53 to 76 percent voter turnout. The hotly contested 1792 race between Governor George Clinton and John Jay drew the most attention. Three-quarters of the town's eligible voters voted. In the 1795 elections George Clinton was no longer a candidate.

In this balloting some 125 men, or 63 percent of those eligible, voted for the governor. The 1798 election again saw John Jay stand. Fifty-seven percent of Newtown's eligible voters voted.[85]

Since both the governor and state senators were elected by the same wealthier constituency in elections held at the same time, the difference in voter turnout between the two is worthy of comment. The three senatorial elections for which voter turnout can be measured ranged between 58 and 81 percent. In 1792, the big race was obviously the governorship. Apparently allegiances were shifting as party organization was just gearing up. Both of these processes generated voter interest. Perhaps substantive fears also played some role in voter participation. Alfred Young suggests that Clintonians publicized John Jay's abolitionist leanings. Townsmen, holding more slaves than any other Queens county town, would have perhaps voted their immediate interest.[86]

Three years later the situation was reversed. In the 1795 state senatorial election a very high 81 percent of eligible townsmen voted. This is one of the few elections in which a townsman ran for statewide office. Benjamin Coe was one of Newtown's political elite. He held town office and was a leading Republican.

The 1798 election resulted in lower voter turnout than in 1795 but still a higher voter participation than in the gubernatorial election. One wonders how attractive to townsmen was the candidacy of Chancellor Robert R. Livingston, owner of the lower manor of Clermont. An aristocrat, Livingston had enjoyed ambivalent support in previous years.[87] On the other hand, DeWitt Clinton, nephew of the popular former governor, owned a country seat in Newtown.

Newtown's interest in state offices can be tracked best through the gubernatorial and senatorial elections. (There is not enough information to say much about the state assembly.) The United States Congress seems to have attracted less interest. A full 60 percent of eligible voters participated in the 1793 election, but this figure is well below the most heavily attended local elections. The returns from 1795 seem low, not only from Newtown but from the other towns as well. Possibly some returns are missing.[88]

By 1795 at least some ideological lines were drawn between as yet latent Democratic Republicans and Federalists. Alfred Young identifies New York Clintonians, who would become Democratic Republicans, as those stressing property and opportunity. This meant that they were anti-taxation and if not pro-slavery, at least anti-abolition. They backed land schemes and in general appealed to the "yeomanry." Newtowners would certainly have appreciated these concerns, being slave-holders but without access to more town lands. They would have supported opening western lands for younger sons. And their Revolutionary experiences would have made them strong supporters of those who protected private property, especially from the demands of the state.[89]

While it is impossible to know exactly why people voted at some times and not at others, Newtown's respectable turnout suggests a knowledgeable and interested electorate. They knew enough about candidates and perhaps about issues to choose when to vote and when to stay home. Though the Newtown of 1800 indulged in national party politics, it was preeminently a part of New York State and its character was influenced by New York City. Among other things, townsmen accepted the

TABLE 4

NEWTOWN VOTING STATISTICS: 1788-1798

Election	Number Eligible	Number Voting[a]	%
1788 State Assembly	270	76	28
1788 Ratifying Convention	270	109	40
1789 Gubernatorial	199	106	53
1792 Gubernatorial	199	151	76
1795 Gubernatorial	199	125	63
1798 Gubernatorial	199	113	57
1792 Senate	199	115	58
1794 Senate	199	171[b]	—
1795 Senate	199	162	81
1798 Senate	199	144	72
1793 U.S. Congress	199	120	60
1795 U.S. Congress	199	66	33

Sources: See text for citations.

a. Where multiple candidates ran, the total vote was divided by the number of voters to get an average number of voters.

b. This total is incomplete because the vote for the fourth candidate was illegible.

urban values of higher education. They subscribed to Union Hall Academy, the major secondary institution of learning on western Long Island. In 1796, Rev. Nathan Woodhull advertised a school "taught by an able instructor, reading, writing, arithmetic, geography, English grammar, Latin, Greek and French." Small farmers would hardly have needed the latter three. Townsmen also advertised for a schoolmaster for the lower grades.[90] And Queens County was becoming a suburb where wealthy New Yorkers, like DeWitt Clinton, erected country seats overlooking the water.

In 1785, Robert Hunter, Jr., a young merchant from London set out on a tour of North American. He noted that "the Island is quite a garden and supplies New York with grain and all kinds of vegetables. Some wheat fields are very forward. The roads are charming, the land well cultivated, and the fences in good order."[91] Ten years later the French exile, Moreau de St. Mery, wrote "there is something singularly picturesque about seeing a large city on one side and truly rural sections on the other. This road is thickly bordered with cherry trees, and passers-by are customarily permitted to pick the fruit which hangs over the road . . . It is planted to crops of Indian corn, wheat, flax, many fruit trees and vegetables . . . This land . . . is high-priced, because the nearness of New York assures a market for all farm products . . . "[92]

The Newtown of 1800 must have looked very much like the Newtown of 1775. Townsmen made their living growing produce and livestock, much of it for the city market. In 1800 there were more orchards and fewer woodlands but the overall sense of a rural agricultural enclave impressed visitors as much after the war as it had before. These farms remained difficult to acquire. Land had long since ceased to be easily available, which meant that newcomers, younger sons and free blacks could rent but not own unless they had capital. New York City, New Jersey and upstate New York, where land became available under Governor Clinton's land policies, would draw younger white males away from Newtown. Neither younger sons nor most new families stayed. Newtown's rate of population growth was far lower than that of New York State as a whole.

Free blacks either left Newtown or were integrated into the households of whites. They seem to have been unable to maintain the independent status suggested in the 1790 census. Slaves continued in bondage until New York State's manumission law of 1799 began the gradual process of abolishing slavery.

The American Revolution made townsmen's lives more difficult and perhaps gave them a taste of real political impotence. However, the evidence fails to suggest either lasting harm or any real change. The major threat during the war years was to property. It is no accident that afterward townsmen supported those committed to property's protection. The Clintonians were probably more attuned to a rural electorate's concerns of this kind. In any case, townsmen supported Clinton and later the Democratic Republicans. They participated in campaigning and a fair number of the many white males who could vote did. However, political behavior had shown itself earlier. It was neither a product of the war nor of newly achieved statehood.

The state constitution of 1777 and the federal Constitution ratified by New York in 1788 allowed Newtowners to continue much as they had before. In that respect, both documents were conservative rather than revolutionary. Edward Countryman has characterized Queens County as a place where "republican independence proved unthinkable."[93] Even though he bases some of his conclusions on Newtown evidence, he uses that material too narrowly. Pre-Revolutionary townsmen declined to participate in provincial affairs not because they felt inferior but because they felt no need. When they were finally faced by developments that clearly affected their interests in 1774, they were the most radical community in the county as they responded to the Continental Congress by electing an extra-legal Committee of Seventeen. Moreover, townsmen would end up representing the county both in the provincial conventions and the new state government until civilian government was restored in 1784. Newtown would continue to be politically aware. It was a willing participant in the new political organizations begun with the birth of the first party system, a system first made possible in the age of the new constitutions.

Notes

1. "Description of New York, Long, and Staten Islands, in 1776," New York Island, September 18, 1776, in William L. Stone, trans., *Letters of Brunswick*

and Hessian Officers During the American Revolution (New York, 1970, reprint of 1891 ed.), 195, 196.

2. Edward Countryman, *A People in Revolution: The American Revolution and Political Society in New York, 1760–1790* (Baltimore and London: The Johns Hopkins University Press, 1981). 105; Jessica Kross, *The Evolution of an American Town: Newtown, New York, 1642–1775* (Philadelphia, 1983), 269-270. For a list of occupations practiced through the seventeenth and eighteenth centuries see Jessica Kross Ehrlich, "A Town Study in Colonial New York: Newtown, Queens County (1642–1790)," (Ph.D. diss., University of Michigan, 1974), Appendix B.

3. For a discussion of land holdings and population see Kross, *Evolution of an American Town* Chapter 8, *passim*, 249. "Names of the Head of Each Family in Newtown in 1771," Manuscripts Collection, Memoria, Riker Collection, New York Public Library, Box 16, vol. 5, 150–152.

4. Countryman, *People in Revolution*, 104–106. The quote is on page 106.

5. The list of assemblymen appears in Patricia U. Bonomi, *A Factious People: Politics and Society in Colonial New York* (New York and London, 1971). Appendix C.

6. Countryman, *People in Revolution*, 108.

7. Henry Onderdonk, Jr., *Documents and Letters Intended to Illustrate the Revolutionary Incidents of Queens County* (New York, 1846), 17–19.

8. The loyal protest appeared in Rivington's *New York Gazetteer*, No. 91 on January 19, 1775. This list and the names of the 100 voters can be found in James Riker, Jr., *The Annals of Newtown* (New York, 1852), 178, 180–181. Queens County's loyalism was publicized by the Provincial Congress at least as early as December 1775. See, for example, the list of "disaffected persons" published in Peter Force,comp, *American Archives*, 4th Ser., 6 vols. (Washington, D. C.: M. St. Clair Clarke and Peter Force, 1837–1853), 4: 372–375. Queens County's reputation as a Tory stronghold has been most recently analyzed by Joseph S. Tiedemann, "A Revolution Foiled: Queens County, New York, 1775–1776," *The Journal of American History* 75 (September 1988), 417–444.

9. For a well-written general description of what happened in Queens County during 1776 see Joseph S. Tiedemann, "Response to Revolution: Queens County, New York, During the Era of the American Revolution" (Ph.D. diss. City University of New York, 1977), chapter 4, *passim*. The quotation is taken from "Description of New York," in Stone, tr., *Letters of Brunswick and Hessian Officers*, 195.

10. For a good short account of the battle of Long Island and subsequent occupation see Myron H. Luke and Robert W. Venables, *Long Island in the American Revolution* (Albany, 1976).

11. Bernard Mason, *The Road to Independence: The Revolutionary Movement in New York, 1773–1777* (Lexington, 1966), 131–133.

12. Ibid., 213, 214. For a good precis of the state constitution see William A. Polf, *The Political Revolution and New York's First Constitution"* (Albany, 1977).

13. Riker, *Annals of Newtown*, 356; Federick Gregory Mather, *The Refugees of 1776 from Long Island to Connecticut* (Albany, 1913), 272, 442, 408, 295.

14. "Firman, Nathan R. 3855." Revolutionary War Pensions and Bounty Land Records. South Carolina Archives Microcopy M804, Reel 977.

15. "Remsen, Garrett R. 8702." Revolutionary War Pensions, Reel 2024.

16. Pre-census population estimates are always tricky. The 1771 census listed about 1,100 whites. Of these roughly half would be male (550) and half of those would be between 16 and 60 (225). The figure of 36 males comes from all sources. The figure of 26 males omits those listed in a survey of properties condemned by the British and reallocated to Loyalist refugees from elsewhere. ("American

Loyalists. Transcript of various Papers relating to the Losses Services and Support of the American Loyalists and to His Majesty's Provincial Forces . . . 1777–1783." 8 vols. Transcribed for the New York Public Library, 1903. 8: 561–564.)

17. Ibid.

18. Tiedemann, "Response to Revolution," 153. "Abstract of Men, Women and Children Victualled at Flushing, Jamaica, Newtown, Denyces Ferry and Brooklyn between 12th & 19th December 1779," Mackenzie papers, The William L. Clements Library, Ann Arbor, Michigan.

19. "Memoranda of the Revolution in Newtown, [1846], Newtown. Queens County, New York," New-York Historical Society, 11, 7.

20. Ibid., *passim.* Onderdonk, *Documents and Letters,* (1846 ed.), 134, 138.

21. Claims, American Loyalists, Public Record Office, Audit Office 12, 110: "Memoranda of the Revolution, "8; Oscar T. Barck, Jr., *New York City During the War for Independence* (Port Washington, N.Y., 1966, reprint of 1931 ed.), 112; "Proceedings of the Board of General Offices of the British Army at New York, 1781," New-York Historical Society, *Collections* 49 (1916), 100–101; Tiedemann, "Response to Revolution," 151–152.

22. Not all historians characterize colonial New York as peaceful and law-abiding. For a discussion of this issue see Kross, *Evolution of an American Town,* 264; "Memoranda of the Revolution," 1, 11, 2; "Minutes of the Court of General Sessions of the Peace and also of Common Pleas," 1722, Queens County Manuscript Records Room, Queens County Court House; Frederick Bernays Wiener, *Civilians Under Military Justice: The British Practice Since 1689, Especially in North America,* (Chicago, 1967), 286.

23. For examples of whaleboat incursions on Long Island see Henry Onderdonk, Jr., *Queens County in Olden Times* (Jamaica, N.Y. 1865), 57–59.

24. The most thorough account of the problems of justice appears in Joseph S. Tiedemann, "Patriots by Default: Queens County, New York, and the British Army, 1776–1783," *William and Mary Quarterly* 43 (January 1986), 35–63.

25. Ibid., 59.

26. Kross, *Evolution of an American Town,* 73, 144, 197. All of the information on town office holding can be found in Ehrlich, "A Town Study in Colonial New York," 56–67. See Table 6 for a summary of office holders between 1776 and 1783. Joseph Tiedemann, "Communities in the Midst of the American Revolution: Queens County, New York, 1774–1775" *Journal of Social History* 28 (Fall 1984), 59.

27. "Memoranda of the Revolution," 12; Onderdonk, *Documents and Letters* (1846 ed.), 132.

28. *Ibid.*, 135–136. There were more than 93 men in town and not everybody signed the letter. Of the 11 possible newcomers, 3 might be townsmen if "Lester" is really "Luyster." Genealogical information from Riker, *Annals of Newtown* fails to list Gilbert, Jacob and Mordecai Lester under the Luyster family, however.

29. Town of Newtown 289. "June 16th 1753. Jacob Reeder Town Clerk. Book of Records," Historical Documents Collection, Queens College, CUNY, Reel TNT 10, 259–267.

30. "Queens County Supervisor's Book [1709–1787]," Museum of the City of New York, 1774, 1775. Hereafter cited as County Minutes.

31. "County Minutes," 1777. Joseph Tiedemann states that the Board of Supervisors ceased to meet after 1780 but the minutes suggest that they continued. "Patriots by Default," 60.

32. Henry Onderdonk, Jr., *Queens County in Olden Times,* 54; Henry Onderdonk, Jr., *Documents and Letters intended to illustrate the Revolutionary Incidents of Queens County, N.Y.* (Hempstead, 1884; reprinted 1976), 30; Onderdonk, *Documents and Letters,* (1846 ed.), 135, 137, 138.

33. Onderdonk, *Queen's County in Olden Times*, 55; Onderdonk, *Documents and Letters*, (1846 ed.), 138, 139.

34. Runaway ads were taken from excerpts from the newspapers compiled by Henry Onderdonk in his various already cited works. A recent work on the subject of slavery and the Revolution in New York is Graham Hodges, "Black Revolt in New York City and the Neutral Zone 1775–1783," unpublished paper. Hodges argues that the war presented slaves with unprecedented new opportunities, including running away.

35. Joseph S. Tiedemann, "Loyalists and Conflict Resolution in Post-Revolutionary New York: Queens County as a Test Case," *New York History* 68 (January 1987), 34. I have identified loyalists through genealogies, "Memoirs of the Revolution," various of the works of Henry Onderdonk, Jr. mentioned elsewhere, Gregory Palmer, *Biographical Sketches of Loyalists of the American Revolution* (Westport, London, 1984), which is an update of Lorenzo Sabine's *Biographical Sketches of the American Revolution* and Esther Clark Wright, *The Loyalists of New Brunswick* (Windsor, N. B., 1955).

36. "Furman, Gabriel," Revolutionary War Pensions, Reel 977, "Firman, Nathan R. 3855." Revolutionary War Pensions, Reel 977, "Riker, Abraham R. 8822." Revolutionary War Pensions, Reel 2048, "Riker, John Berrien W. 4321." Revolutionary War Pensions, Reel 2048; Riker, *Annals of Newtown*, 356, 286, 313.

37. "Names of the Head of Each Family in Newtown in 1771;" "Return of the Tax List of the township of Newtown, Queens County New York, MSS.," New-York Historical Society; "Schedule of the Whole Number of Persons Contained within the County of Queens. Township of Newtown," "Schedules of the Second Census of the United States 1800," National Archives, Reel 32:25, 60–63A. I have excluded women and absentee owners from the list for the purposes of this analysis. Of the 102 absent from the 1784 list, 38 are known to have died. These deaths are 54 percent of known deaths. If those for whom there is no death date died at the same pre-1784/post-1784 ratio as those for whom there is information, then the number of those who died rises to 55.

38. "Names of the Head of Each Family in Newtown in 1771"; "Return of the Tax List of the township of Newtown [1784]." All genealogical information was taken from Riker, *Annals of Newtown*, Second Part, "Its Genealogical History."

39. "Names of the Head of Each Family in Newtown in 1771"; "Return of the Tax List of the township of Newtown [1784]"; Onderdonk, *Queens County in Olden Times*, 67.

40. *Return of the Whole Number of Persons within the Several Districts of the United States* (Philadelphis, 1791) facsimile ed., 36.

41. All figures are taken from the 1790 and 1800 census schedules. Genealogical materials are from Riker *Annals* and various church and probate records. The figure for male deaths was calculated. There are 24 known deaths between 1790 and 1800 out of a total of 87 known deaths or 27.5 percent. Assuming that those not known are in the same proportion as those known and using a population of 242 yields 242 x 27.5 or 67 deaths.

42. "Schedule of the Whole Number of Persons Contained within the County of Queens. Township of *Newtown*, [1800]." There are two free black household heads on page 60[a] which are obliterated. *Return of the Whole Number of Persons within the Several Districts of the United States* (Washington, [1801]), 27.

43. Population growth rates can be measured in various ways. I have chosen the simplest, which assumes a steady arithmetic rate of growth according to the formula $r = [(P_2 - P_1)/P_1]/10$. Population figures for Newtown came from various published and unpublished censuses. 1790 figures were taken from *Returns of the Whole Number of Persons Within the Several Districts of the United States* (Philadelphia, 1791), 36. The *Return of the Whole Number of Per-*

sons within the Several Districts of the United States (Washington, D. C., 1801), 27, had too many errors in the free male totals to be usable. The figures for 1800 are from the "Schedule of the Whole Number of Persons contained within the County of Queens: Township of Newtown, [1800]." This census is not completely legible and therefore some of my figures may be off. I calculated a population of 2,224 while the census states that it was 2,225. The error may lie in the slave population. "County of Queens, Population Schedules of the Third Census of the United States 1810," National Archives, Reel 252:34, 274–288. New York State figures are found in U. S. Bureau of the Census, *Historical Statistics of the United States: Colonial Times to 1970* (Washington, D. C., 1975), 1:32.

44. Three of the surnames among the 324 are illegible. There are also seven households where the full name is illegible. These have been excluded from figures given here although the census shows that two of these households belonged to free blacks.

45. *Return of the Whole Number of Persons* [1791], 36.

46. Sex ratios were calculated from the 1800 and 1810 manuscript census schedules.

47. Tench Coxe, *A Statement of the Arts and Manufactures of the United States of America for the Year 1810* (Philadelphia, 1814), 32–38.

48. For a discussion of "young" and "old" populations see Henry S. Shryock et al, *The Methods and Materials of Demography* (Washington, D. C.: Department of Commerce, Bureau of the Census, 1975) rev. ed., vol 1, 234. Newtown's death rate was far lower than modern underdeveloped nations. For example, the number of people in Puerto Rico aged fifty and over had not yet reached 14 percent by 1960. The United States percentage for those over 50 was just under 14 percent in 1900 and was comparable to Newtown's by 1920. (Ibid., 236.)

49. Information of the three white males living alone is from a multitude of sources including Riker, *Annals*. The 1790 census shows no free blacks living with whites. The 1800 census shows 41 free blacks living with whites.

50. The discrepancy in the number of slaves occurs because of illegible or destroyed parts of the manuscript census schedule. The 512 slaves were listed in the published 1800 schedule. The 508 were the number I could actually find in the manuscript census.

51. *Laws of the State of New York* 23rd Session (Albany, 1799), 721; "Town Book 289," 290, 292, 294, 296.

52. *Greenleaf's New York Journal, & Patriotic Register,* January 1, January 11, 1794.

53. "Minute Book." It is unclear what accounts for the rise in the 1784 tax list. These are assessed values and a higher rate of assessment, possible since a special tax was levied in 1784, would result in the higher figure. "Return of the Tax List of the township of Newtown [1784]." Vertical distribution of Newtown's wealth can be compared with that of Chester County, Pennsylvania, a place which was not controlled by an occupying army the way Newtown was. The similarities between the two distributions are striking and perhaps suggest a larger rural pattern. For this comparison see Ehrlich, "A Town Study in Colonial New York," 163–164. The Chester County data is in James T. Lemon and Gary B. Nash, "The Distribution of Wealth in Eighteenth-Century Chester County, Pennsylvania, 1693–1803," rep. in *Class and Society in Early America,* ed. Gary B. Nash (Englewood Cliffs, 1970), 177.

54. Polf, *Political Revolution and New York's First Constitution,* 50, 51, 53. The 1795 census is found in the *Journal of the Assembly of the State of New York,* 19th Session, (New York, 1796), 31. Since the census did not give the number of males 21 and over but males 16 and over I have used Alfred Young's formula that 80 percent of all males over 16 would be 21 or over. [Alfred Young,

The Democratic Republicans of New York: The Origins 1763–1797 (Chapel Hill, 1967), 587, n21.

55. The 1808 census is in the *Journal of the Senate of the State of New York*, 31st Session (Albany, 1808), 130–131. Using the 1800 census and assuming that those between 16 and 25 are evenly distributed by age shows a total of 369 men over 21. This figure is probably a bit high since those leaving would more likely be in the 21-to-25 age bracket than in the 16-to-20 age bracket.

56. Coxe, *A Statement of the Arts and Manufactures of the United States of America*, 32-38.

57. *The Daily Advertiser: Political, Historical, and Commercial*, February 8, 1787; *Greenleaf's New York Journal, & Patriotic Register*, March 15, 1794, February 5, 1796.

58. "County Minutes," 1777, 1778: "Town Book 289," 278, 282, 284, 286, 293. For work on New York's poor see Robert E. Cray, Jr., *Paupers and Poor Relief in New York City and Its Rural Environs, 1700–1830* (Philadelphia, 1988).

59. "Town Book 289," 288, 293, 300, 303. Cray, *Paupers and Poor Relief*, 94-99.

60. "Town Book 289," 297-298.

61. Genealogical materials are taken from Riker, *Annals of Newtown*; office holders were found in "Town Book 289" from 1760 to 1800.

62. "Extracts from Minutes of the Court of Assize of Queens Co. 1722–1787," from *"Long Island in Olden Times*, compiled by Henry Onderdonk, Jr., (Jamaica, L. I., 1870), Brooklyn Historical Society, 43.

63. Onderdonk, *Queens County in Olden Times*, 66. For a listing of various suits see Onderdonk, *Documents and Letters* (1884 ed.), 64–65; Palmer, *Biographical Sketches of Loyalists*, 886. The price of the Van Dyne farm came from Onderdonk, *Queens County in Olden Days*, 67. Tiedemann also notes that few estates were confiscated ("Loyalists and Conflict Resolution," 36). For Thomas McFarren see John Thomas Reilly, "The Confiscation and Sale of the Loyalist Estates and Its Effect Upon the Democratization of Landholding in New York State: 1779–1800" (Ph. D. diss. Fordham University, 1974), 245-246.

64. Riker, *Annals of Newtown*, 224; Onderdonk, *Documents and Letters* (1884 ed.), 65.

65. Countryman, *A People in Revolution*, Part III.

66. Tiedemann, "Patriots by Default," 35-63; Tiedemann, "Loyalists and Conflict Resolution," 42-43; Onderdonk, *Queens County in Olden Times*, 68.

67. For New York City see Mary O'Connor English, "New York in Transition, 1783–1786" (Ph.D. Diss. Fordham University, 1971). I should like to thank Dr. Jack Meyer of the History Department, University of South Carolina for pointing out the relative civility of eighteenth-century warfare. As John Shy notes, the outcome might have been much different if General Charles Lee, who advocated what we now call guerrilla warfare, had prevailed. See "American Strategy: Charles Lee and the Radical Alternative," in John Shy, *A People Numerous and Armed* (London, Oxford, and New York, 1976), 132-162.

68. Countryman, *People in Revolution*, 162. Assemblymen are identified in Appendix 2.

69. Most of the returns used here come from Onderdonk, *Queens County in Olden Times*, 71, 73, 82, 84, 88. Others come from *Greenleaf's New York Journal & Patriotic Register*, June 7, 1794, May 30, 1795. Many of the returns given in the newspapers were by county or for the Southern District and not by town.

70. Onderdonk, *Queens County in Olden Times*, 71; Stephen L. Schechter, "A Biographical Gazetteer of New York Federalists and Antifederalists," in Stephen L. Schechter, ed., *The Reluctant Pillar: New York and the Adoption of the Federal Constitution* (Troy, N.Y., 1985), 197-198.

71. Robert Ernst, "The Long Island Delegates and the New York Ratifying Convention," *New York History* 70 (January 1989), 55.

72. Ibid., 57; Onderdonk, *Queens County in Olden Times*, 71.

73. Riker, *Annals of Newtown*, 232; *Return of the Whole Number of Persons* [1791]; "Schedule of the Whole Number of Persons Contained within the County of Queens. Township of *Newtown*" [1800]; "County of Queens, Population Schedules of the Third Census of the United States 1810"; *The Papers of Alexander Hamilton*, ed. Harold C. Syrett and Jacob E. Cooke, 27 vols. (New York and London, 1961-1987) 5: 261, 262n.

74. Ernst, "Long Island Delegates," 57; Schechter, "Biographical Gazetteer, 197-198.

75. Onderdonk, *Queens County in Olden Times*, 73, 80, 88; *Greenleaf's New York Journal, & Patriotic Register*, May 30, 1795.

76. Ernst, "Long Island Delegates," 58-59; Onderdonk, *Queens County in Olden Times*, 80.

77. Young, *Democratic Republicans*, 49, 253, 333; *Greenleaf's New York Journal, & Patriotic Register*, June 7, 1794, May 30, 1795; Ernst, "Long Island Delegates," 58-59; Countryman, *A People in Revolution*, 211.

78. Onderdonk, *Queens County in Olden Times*. 82, 84; Ernst, "The Long Island Delegates." 63-67. The Jones quote is on 67.

79. Ernst, "The Long Island Delegates," 71.

80. Onderdonk, *Queens County in Olden Times*, 81-82.

81. Ibid., 82; Young, *Democratic Republicans*, 279. The assemblymen from Queens County in 1793 were Jacob Hicks, Whitehead Cornell, and Samuel Clowes.

82. Onderdonk, *Queens County in Olden Times*, 89.

83. Onderdonk, *Queens County in Olden Times*, 17: Linda Grant DePauw, *The Eleventh Pillar: New York State and the Federal Constitution* (Ithaca, N.Y., 1966), 157.

84. Onderdonk, *Queens Count in Olden Times*, 71; DePauw, *The Eleventh Pillar*, 149, 157. The percentage for Queens County was calculated from DePauw's figures of 3,109 potential voters and 934 actual voters.

85. Onderdonk, *Queens County in Olden Times*, 80, 88; *Greenleaf's New York Journal, & Patriotic Register*, May 30, 1795.

86. Young, *Democratic Republicans*, 286-289.

87. Ibid., 434.

88. *Greenleaf's New York Journal, & Patriotic Register*, May 30, 1795.

89. Alfred Young, *Democratic Republicans*, 54, 55, 238, 302.

90. Onderdonk, *Queens County in Olden Times*,, 85, 87.

91. *Quebec to Carolina in 1785–1786: Being the Travel Diary and observations of Robert Hunter, Jr., a Young Merchant of London* ed. Louis B. Wright and Marion Tinling (San Marino, California, 1943), 139.

92. *Moreau de St. Mery's American Journal [1793–1798]*, trans. and ed. Kenneth Roberts and Anna M. Roberts (Garden City, N.Y. 1947), 172.

93. Countryman, *People in Revolution*, 108.

Philipse Manor Hall in Yonkers. Courtesy of Historic Hudson Valley, Tarrytown, New York. Gift of La Duchesse de Talleyrand.

Manorial Influence in New York After the American Revolution

Jacob Judd

In Dixon Ryan Fox's famous study, *The Decline of Aristocracy in the Politics of New York,* the presumption was made that the aristocracy's loss of political control could be traced to Thomas Jefferson's victory in the disputed presidential election of 1800. In actuality, aristocratic influence, as such, had been losing force within New York since the days of the American Revolution. As early as the opening years of the 1770s, powerful landlords no longer could predict with any degree of certainty which course their tenants would take in the preliminary stages of the Revolutionary movement.[1] Middling farmers or urban dwellers chose to be loyal to the crown or to take active part in the rebellion as their individual circumstances influenced them. Their decisions were made, in many instances, without a direct relationship to political positions assumed by the great and economically powerful landlords. Proprietary control of election results within their landed jurisdictions were coming to an end with the legislative elections of 1768–1769. Within a few years no one could safely predict the outcomes of local elections even where the most prominent landholders held sway. Furthermore, throughout that period, former faceless local inhabitants began to serve with increasing numbers on local boards and in minor elective positions. Landlord control was slipping away by a combination of political and economic forces beyond their grasp.[2]

The newly found and hard won political voice would not easily be squandered away by this rising element once political independence had been won from England. An independent state government offered these yeomen places in government that were previously assumed to be beyond their reach. Such improved political status did not come easily; it had been bitterly fought for and would not be carelessly surrendered.

One can question the extent of proprietary dominance over the tenants as far as political control was concerned. We need not belabor the point that the language contained in manorial grants pertaining to rights and privileges of the manor lord had no actual relationship to practice. While the form and substance of these early grants had more in common with English medieval practices, actuality found an entirely different set of relationships. No courts leet or baron were ever established, and in no instance did the word of the manorial lord have the force of law. Power came through control of land relationships: terms of lease or sale, the right of repossession, determination of values attributed to improvements, and through the landlord's role in the sale and transportation of agricultural products.[3]

The concept of a manorial lordship is more a figment of the romantic concepts of nineteenth-century local historians than an expression of fact. A case in point is two major manors in Westchester County, Philipsburg and Van Cortlandt. On the Philipsburg Manor, the lands were held in entail through succeeding generations from the late 1600s until the Revolutionary War. The title "Lord" technically existed throughout that time. At no time, however, in either official records relating to the Philipses or in the scattered manuscripts which may be directly attributed to the Philipses themselves was the title Lord of the Manor ever used. Throughout the 1750s and 1760s, when local elections were held on the Manor, whenever Frederick Philipse's name appeared on the records, he was simply designated as "esq." Furthermore, while Frederick Philipse III was elected supervisor in 1752, he does not appear to have been reelected. In the meanwhile, local freemen were serving as constables, clerks, assessors, fence viewers, pound masters, and road overseers.

The lands of Van Cortlandt Manor, from the 1730s onward, were distributed among many close and distant relatives. The Lordship as such vanished with these land divisions. Van Cortlandt Manor was one of two in the Province of New York that had the special privilege of sending its own representative to the general assembly. Until 1768 the possessor of that seat was a Ver Planck rather than a Van Cortlandt. As for elections held during those years on the Manor, they were under the supervision of several freeholders, and there is no evidence pointing to Van Cortlandt family members either manipulating election procedures or their results.[4]

If political control existed on these vast estates, then it should have been a simple task to predict where tenant sentiments lay at the time of the Revolutionary movement by examining the attitudes of the manor holders. Such was not the case. There was no way of foretelling the eventual allegiance of the tenants on either Philipsburg or Van Cortlandt manors. Of the two landholders, Frederick Philipse III would be eventually attainted of treason, while Pierre Van Cortlandt emerged as the first lieutenant governor of the independent State of New York. Their tenants proved just as divergent in thought and deed. Loyalist contingents were organized from the tenantry of both estates, and the same tenantry also provided numbers of volunteers for the Continental forces.

Tenant reactions emanated from individualistic philosophies, from a particular outlook on life and, perhaps, were simply expedient. Of the two Westchester landholders, the Philipse family had proved far more generous than the Van Cortlandts in their tenant lease arrangements. The Philipses had not raised land rents for over a decade, and in a number of instances had not even collected rents from some tenants for almost the same period of time. The Van Cortlandts, meanwhile, were assiduous in their rent collecting. Frederick Philipse III became a loyalist; Pierre Van Cortlandt, an ardent Revolutionary. The tenantry of both manors was divided in its loyalties. The tenants apparently determined their own political positions irrespective of the affiliations of their landlords or of their own landholding arrangements.[5]

If this, in brief, has demonstrated that tenants were developing their own independent thought patterns, why then should one suppose that an issue of such consequence as the ratifying of the Federal Constitution should not follow suit? It may be also noted that with victory in the struggle for separation from the mother country came a revolutionary reaction which was expressed in the adoption of measures that called for the breaking up of estates previously held by loyalists. The political power of such families as the Philipses, De Lanceys, and Johnsons was brought to an end as their land holdings were made available to worthy former tenants and others who made purchases through the commissioners of forfeiture. Of course, as always, those closely affiliated with the power structure seemed to obtain some of the choicest parcels. Gerard G. Beekman, Jr., a New York City merchant, was able to acquire prime Westchester County property along the Pocantico River—a major portion of the former Philipsburg Manor holdings. Beekman was a relatively unknown merchant, but his wife, Cornelia, just happened to be the sister of Philip Van Cortlandt, the commissioner of forfeiture. After Gerard's death, Cornelia turned to real estate development and helped to create Beekmantown.

The great upriver landholders, the Van Rensselaer and Livingston families, had been a major force in provincial politics. They controlled vast landholdings, yet at no particular time could it be stated that their tenants followed their political leadership with blind faith. While both family leaders became revolutionaries, their estates produced loyalist adherents during the conflict, and it does not seem that they were able to exert any overt influence on their estates following the war's conclusion. While these landlords may have been revolutionaries in sentiment, we also know that they did not particularly appreciate the actions of those tenants who sought a greater voice in their own local affairs or a chance to possess property outright in their own names. Individual motivations and actions are quite complex; reactions cannot be attributed to any one set of motives or philosophies at a given moment.

With the adoption of a state constitution in 1777, newly independent New York was provided with an opportunity to test governmental formats wherein the populace could exert a greater influence in local affairs. With the expansion of town governments in the 1780s governmental positions were created in local officialdom and were subsequently filled by freeholders in the communities. Once such a foothold was established for local government, it became almost impossible to dislodge a coterie of minor officials or to sway them from the principle of closely held governmental control.

It is less necessary to assess the reasons why New Yorkers were somewhat interested in modifying the Articles of Confederation than to explain why they would more logically oppose a stronger centralized government. Statement after statement came forth, during the period of gestation between the drafting and final ratification of the Constitution, to the effect that throughout the entire history of western civilization only those governments which had been organized and controlled by and for a local constituency had survived. The idea was ridiculed that one government could supervise and act for the general welfare of a citizenry stretched over thousands of miles and so diverse in culture, tradition, and economy. History has taught an important political lesson, they argued, that only closely controlled governments have survived. Furthermore, a revolution had just been fought, at a high cost in lives and property, for the purpose of removing a governmental structure which had tried to regulate its far-flung colonial possessions from a distance of over 3,000 miles. That imperial power lost control, many pointed out, because they had not heeded the lessons of history. Were the New Yorkers now going to knowingly aid in the recreation of such a governmental structure? Hopefully not. This argument was accompanied by a growing opposition to the movement for the creation of a more powerful body distantly located from the geographically confined constituencies.[6]

As of the late 1780s, great landholders of New York may be divided into two geographic units: those whose economic well-being was tied to the commercial center of New York City and its superb harbor facilities; and those whose interests were more attuned to lumbering, the fur trade, and various mercantile activities, for which Albany was the urban hub. An important historical assumption may be postulated that, almost from the earliest Dutch days of occupation, a variation had appeared in outlook, in economic attitudes, and even in the way of life between the southern and northern areas of the province. While some have cast doubt that such a distinction really had an impact on the vote for ratification, nevertheless it is worth examining.[7]

New York City, with its year round harbor facilities, had a mercantilistic interest that extended far beyond its immediate economic hinterland. While most merchants were quite content to reestablish their local business connections following the close of the Revolution, a group of city merchants were engaged in opening a trade with far off China. Their visionary outlook assumed international proportions even at the early stage. In order to carry such concepts forward, it would be necessary to have a strong government that was capable of protecting the sea lanes through which their vessels would ply. They needed a unified currency that would have some standing in both domestic and foreign markets. There were myriad economic reasons why such merchants would be in support of a centralized governmental structure that could offer them the level of protection for the economic opportunities they sought. Their hinterland, on the other hand, was composed primarily of agricultural regions which did not as yet see the advantages to be gained by instituting major changes in the existing governmental relationship. The farmers and small landholders of the surrounding countryside were more involved in meeting their immediate debt obligations, in sending their produce to market, and, perhaps, in expanding their lands at a propitious time.

In the New York regions to the north and west of the major harbor, the great landowners envisioned expanded trade opportunities for their locally produced crops in a fashion similar to that of the New York City merchants. Quite frequently, these great landowners were major players in the commercial life of New York City or were closely involved through family or partnership arrangements. The farmers, both the freemen and tenants, had immediate goals which did not include the expansionary dreams of the leading merchants or landowners. Such farm owners sought a stable government that was attuned to the needs of the citizenry. To many, the existing Confederation seemed to be adequate. It perhaps needed some minor modifications, but it appeared to be serving their needs.

In the present-day era of thirty-second television commercials espousing political causes or candidates, it is somewhat difficult to envision a major political decision being made on the basis of a series of anonymous editorials appearing in weekly newspapers. The struggle over ratification of the 1787 Constitution, while producing magnificent commentaries on political philosophy and government in the form of such newspaper articles, did not, it seems, create major political confrontations within most of New York's counties. Again, while the large landowners seemed to support ratification, as a group they did not make overt political efforts to win converts to their cause. They perhaps assumed that New York would have to ratify, sooner or later, and they were therefore willing to bide their time. It does not, however, appear that their lack of organized activity stemmed primarily from lethargy.

The election for delegate seats to New York's ratifying convention was carried out on a county by county basis. Manor holdings and other major real estate units were subsumed under a countywide umbrella. Consequently, election results were reported on a county basis and not by real property divisions. Counties that contained some of the largest landed estates—Columbia, Dutchess, Montgomery, and Ulster—all eventually supported Antifederalist delegates for the state's ratification convention. John P. Kaminski, in his excellent essay, "New York: The Reluctant Pillar," provides us with a detailed account of the activities of some of the major landholders during this election campaign.[8] Basically, such men as Philip Schuyler, Stephen Van Rensselaer, Brockholst Livingston, Robert R. Livingston, and their political cohorts confined their politicizing to writing occasional letters exhorting others to get out the vote in favor of Federalist supporters of the Constitution. In each of those counties, Antifederalists carried the day.

On the basis of voting behavior exhibited by members of the state's legislature in the years between 1784 and 1787, particular counties could be regarded as supporters of Governor George Clinton and his stance toward having political power remain under individual state control in contrast to those who, as early as 1784, sought major revisions in the Articles of Confederation. On such politically sensitive issues relating to paper money, a federal impost, loyalist political activities, and election of delegates to the Constitutional Convention, the counties of New York, Albany, Kings, Richmond, and Suffolk were held to be anti-Clintonian in sentiment. The remaining counties of Westchester, Orange, Dutchess, Ulster, Washington, Montgomery, and Queens could be regarded as safely in the Clintonian corner. Columbia County's position was as yet a cipher.[9]

John Kaminski notes that Columbia County contained a major portion of the Livingston clan's properties. The members of that notable family were expected to do all in their power to obtain support for Federalist candidates. Peter Van Schaack, a Federalist candidate, would write that "We have some very great men among us, and a wonderful degree of information among the common people." There also appears to have been varying differences of opinion, for Van Schaack also reported that "a few bloody noses have been in consequence." That the campaign was not going as well as originally thought was soon stated by Federalist Philip Schuyler when he commented to Chancellor Robert R. Livingston that "all was in confusion there."[10] When election time approached, it was assumed that Livingston Manor would be so strongly Federalist that it could withstand the Antifederalist strength in the other communities within the county. Assumptions notwithstanding, Columbia sent three Antifederalist delegates to the convention.

Westchester was regarded as a safe Antifederalist county. Throughout the 1780s it consistently voted with the Clintonian bloc. Furthermore, New York's lieutenant governor was Pierre Van Cortlandt, owner and manager of the vast family holdings in Westchester County. Pierre Van Cortlandt's political career had been closely associated with that of Governor Clinton ever since the early days of the Revolutionary movement in New York. It was assumed that Westchester could be counted on to continue its strong support for Clinton's and Van Cortlandt's political views. Interestingly, the lieutenant governor's son, Philip Van Cortlandt, would assume a role contrary to that of his father's. Philip had served in the Continental Army and was a breveted brigadier general. Following the ousting of the British, Philip returned to civilian life and was named one of two commissioners of forfeiture for the State of New York. In that capacity he oversaw the breakup of confiscated loyalist estates and the subsequent sale of those lands. While at the Continental Army's last encampment at New Windsor, New York, Philip joined a number of fellow officers to form the organization, the Society of the Cincinnati. Comprising the leading military officers, including George Washington, the society continued into peacetime as a lobbying agency for veteran's pensions and land grants. There is strong evidence to demonstrate that the founding members of the society proved to be Federalist in sentiment. This is understandable as a point of view in keeping with their efforts to obtain compensation and recognition for their patriotic services, and with their experiences in dealing with individual state organizations throughout the war years.[11]

Therefore, when the election campaign for delegates to the ratifying convention was instituted in Westchester County, Philip soon emerged as a Federalist advocate. In March 1788,

Leonard Gansevoort could declare that Philip Van Cortlandt had emerged "as out of a Gothic Cloister, with the Air so strongly impregnated with federalism has infused into his nostrils the aromatic, his whole frame infected with the contagion has called him forth to Action and has transported him from extreme inaction to increasing exertion. [H]e is making Interest to be returned a Delegate and from the Influence which his Office as Commissioner of forfeiture has acquired him and his established reputation for probity and Integrity will doubtless insure him success. [H]ow it will go with the Members he is supporting in general is very uncertain, the People have in general a tincture of antifederalism. [T]ho' it is said that six States having already adopted the Constitution stifles in great Measure the latent sparks."[12]

There is not one reference to this campaign in the correspondence of either of the Van Cortlandts, father or son. A supposition may be presented whereby Pierre, the lieutenant governor, having to remain silent on this issue or else severely antagonize Governor George Clinton, permitted his son to state the position which both may have ardently sought. Be that as it may, Philip's slate turned out to be the victorious one. Philip had agreed to run on a Federalist slate which also included Philip Livingston, Lewis Morris of the Manor of Morrisania, Lott Sarles, Richard Hatfield and Thaddeus Crane. Arrayed against them were such veteran office holders as Philip Pell, who was the Sheriff of Westchester County, Jonathan Tompkins, Abijah Gilbert, Thomas Thomas, Joseph Strang and Samuel Drake.

The election, opened to all white males twenty-one years of age or older, was held from April 29 to May 2. While there were some 4,408 males eligible to vote, only 1,093 actually took part in this important election. To the surprise and delight of the Federalists, their candidates swept the election. A Federalist from Westchester was reported in a New York newspaper as having said, "the *Federalist Ticket*. . . has prevailed by a majority of two to one. So decisive a victory, I frankly confess, has exceeded my most sanguine expectations."[13] The highest Federalist vote numbered 694 against an Antifederalist vote of 399. Westchester had surprised everyone by moving away from an adherence to Clinton's point of view to one of federalism.

There were also upsets in Albany and Suffolk Counties, both of which turned Antifederal, while Kings County supported a

Federalist ticket. Only four counties voted Federalist—New York, Westchester, Richmond, Kings. As a result, Antifederalist representatives were given a predominent lead, 46 to 19 in the ratifying convention. With so many Antifederalists having had careers in practical politics before reaching this convention, it should not come as a surprise that enough of them were eventually persuaded that political reality and practicality would necessitate a change of heart for some, to the extent that a sufficient number would join the Federalist chorus and support ratification. Their support was accompanied by the caveat that the new governmental structure initiate the necessary procedures by which various modifications could be made to the document now ratified. Their call for such action, coupled with those emanating from Massachusetts and Virginia proved sufficient for the First Congress to adopt a series of amendments which were then sent to the states for ratification. Out of this sequence of activities emerged our Bill of Rights.

Manorial land divisions retained relevancy only in the realm of a landlord-tenant relationship that continued well into the nineteenth century. As for maintaining a political domination over their tenants by the so-called manorial lords, that concept had long ceased to have any actual relevance. While such great landholders as the Livingstons, Schuylers, Van Cortlandts, and Van Rensselaers may have continued their earlier important political roles in provincial and later national affairs, their domination of localized political activity, as much or little as it may have been, was a thing of the past. Perhaps, as their sights became set on higher offices in the land, they lost particular interest in the politics actively flourishing in their own backyards.

Notes

1. Dixon Ryan Fox in *The Decline of Aristocracy in the Politics of New York* (New York, 1919), emphasized the diminished role played by the elite in state politics and was not concerned with what was occurring at the local level. The first examination of changes taking place at the grass roots was Alfred F. Young's *The Democratic Republicans of New York: The Origins, 1763–1797* (Chapel Hill, N.C., 1967). Young was particularly interested in the role played by yeomen and tenant farmers in the ratification controversy. See especially pages 85–94.

2. See, for example, Sung Bok Kim, *Landlord and Tenant in Colonial New*

York: Manorial Society, 1664–1775 (Chapel Hill, N.C., 1978). Focusing on manors in Westchester County, the author analyzes the economic and political relationships which developed on those manors.

3. Ibid.; and Jacob Judd, ed., *Correspondence of the Van Cortlandt Family of Cortlandt Manor, 1748–1800* (Tarrytown, N.Y., 1977), *passim.*

4. Judd, *Van Cortlandt Family,* 4–9, 512–516, 531–532.

5. Jacob Judd, "Frederick Philipse III of Westchester County: A Reluctant Loyalist," in *The Loyalist Americans: A Focus on Greater New York,* Robert A. East and Jacob Judd, eds. (Tarrytown, N.Y., 1975), 25–43.

6. An excellent collection of New York Antifederalist writings may be found in Cecilia Kenyon, ed., *The Antifederalists* (New York, 1966), 301–405. A brief discussion of their points of view is found in Jackson T. Main's *The Antifederalists: Critics of the Constitution 1781–1788* (New York, 1961), 233–242.

7. DePauw, *Eleventh Pillar,* 27–33; and Main, *The Antifederalists,* 47–50.

8. John P. Kaminski, "New York: The "Reluctant Pillar," in *The Reluctant Pillar: New York and the Adoption of the Federal Constitution,* Stephen L. Schechter, ed. (Troy, N.Y., 1985). This essay develops and analyses themes briefly covered in the pioneering work by Linda Grant DePauw, *The Eleventh Pillar: New York State and the Federal Constitution* (Ithaca, N.Y., 1966).

9. William B. Michaelson, "Westchester Ratifies the Constitution," *The Westchester Historian,* 64(Fall, 1988), 108–112; Kaminski, "Reluctant Pillar," 93–98.

10. Kaminski, "Reluctant Pillar," 93–98.

11. This is discussed by Edwin G. Burrows, "Military Experience and the Origins of Federalism and Anti-Federalism," in Jacob Judd and Irwin H. Polishook, eds., *Aspects of Early New York Society and Politics* (Tarrytown, N.Y., 1974), 83–92.

12. As cited in Kaminski, "Reluctant Pillar," 98.

13. Ibid.

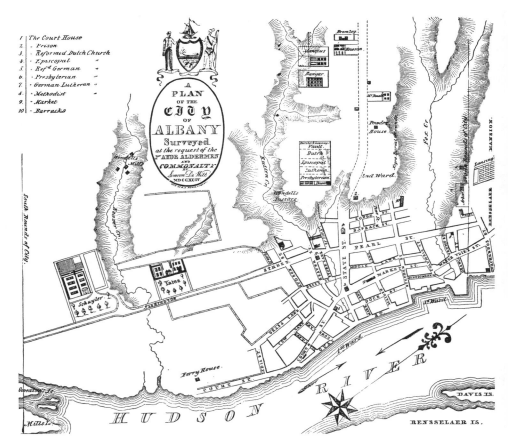

The Court House
Prison
Reformed Dutch Church
Episcopal
Ref'd German
Presbyterian
German Lutheran
Methodist
Market
Barracks

The eastern wards of Albany. This version of Simeon de Witt's 1794 map was published in Weise's The History of the City of Albany, New York *(1884).*

Episodes in the Coming of Age of an Early American Community: Albany, N.Y., 1780–1793

Stefan Bielinski

EPISODE 1: The new year of 1780 opened on a particularly bitter winter. On January 4, the state government was to convene in Albany for the first time, but sub-zero temperatures and an "amazing Body of Snow" kept Governor George Clinton from addressing the legislature at the Albany city hall until January 27. With New York City occupied by the British, and Poughkeepsie, Kingston, and the other mid-Hudson villages so vulnerable to British assault, upriver Albany represented a welcome haven for the war-weary revolutionaries who had been forced to lead a "government on the run" since 1776. Although the legislature sat in a number of other locations before settling permanently in Albany in 1797, New York's second city was ideally situated to accommodate a new state that was spreading hundreds of miles north and west for the first time. Founded as a trading post in 1624, geographically-favored Albany had evolved into a regional commercial and service center that by 1780 had outgrown its colonial shell and was undergoing a major adaptive change of its own.

Attracted to the meetings at the crowded city hall were Stephen Lush—the governor's secretary; Stewart Dean—a noted mariner; James Caldwell—a manufacturing innovator; Edward Compston—a just-retired Massachusetts army officer about to begin a business career; and a number of other educated and talented opportunists whose business had brought them to Albany. Missing the proceedings were Philip Schuyler, Abraham

Ten Broeck, John Lansing Jr., James Stevenson, Abraham C. Cuyler, and also most of the young men who composed the rank and file of the community. These native sons had been caught up in the war. Leaving wives and mothers to tend their Albany homes, they were the actual combatants—although not everyone wound up on the same side.[1]

Episode 2: Late in 1785, Stewart Dean and his partners sold their sloop, the *Experiment*, to a larger group of investors who selected Dean to sail the vessel to China. Loaded with naval products, spirits, furs, and carrying 18,000 Spanish dollars, the tiny *Experiment* reached Canton where Dean was able to barter his cargo for tea and porcelain, which were in great demand and short supply in America. Returning to New York in April of 1787, he settled accounts with his Manhattan-based investors and came home to Albany where, an already-distinguished sailor, he was feted and was honored by the naming of a riverside street to recognize his achievement. Over the previous century-and-a-half, more than a hundred ships like the *Experiment* had been built by Albany artisans. Owned by the city's merchants, these useful vessels were primarily engaged in carrying country products to New York where they were exchanged for items imported from Europe. But since the break with Great Britain, the Albany fleet increasingly made for foreign ports on its own.[2]

Episode 3: On August 8, 1788, all of Albany turned out to watch a gala parade celebrating ratification of the Federal Constitution. At sunrise, the marchers formed in the fields north of the city. Led by Peter Gansevoort's troop of horse, they paraded through Albany's main streets spurred on by salutes, toasts, and general cheering. The procession featured the members of the Albany corporation—the "city fathers," officers of the state government, clergymen, jurists, professional men, military officers, and all of Albany's notables including traditional leaders such as Major General Philip Schuyler, who displayed a parchment copy of the Constitution, and Stephen Van Rensselaer, the young Patroon, who carried an "elegant plough" to symbolize agriculture. After these peacocks, came the body of the community's tradesmen, craftsmen, artisans, and other working men—organized by function, from axemen to weavers. None of the accounts of the festivities noted any women marchers. No fewer than forty specific production activities were represented, each by a contingent in a carriage, wagon, or on foot carrying banners proclaiming "Success to American Manufactures" and "May our exports exceed our imports."

As the parade turned up State Street, its way was blocked by a group of disgruntled antifederalists who, after a brief exchange of name calling, punching, and rock throwing, were scattered by Gansevoort's cavalry. During the skirmish, James Caldwell, the manufacturer who was marching in the company of glassmakers, was struck in the head with a brick. Was the beaning of this newcomer accidental or did it represent a "rough music" response to the changes that already were transforming this traditional community into a modern city?[3]

Episode 4: Downtown Albany was stirred from its Sunday evening slumber by the screams of "fire." Flames spread from a stable owned by Leonard Gansevoort to consume most of the buildings on the block of North Market Street bounded by State Street, Middle Alley, and Maiden Lane. The blaze was kept from engulfing the entire old city area by the initiative of two pillars of the community. Rector Thomas Ellison directed the gathering crowd in dousing the still unscathed Pearl Street buildings with water, passed along from nearby wells in buckets to fill the city pumpers, while Captain Edward Willet ordered his crew to chop and clear a number of frame structures, thus forming a fire break. Later, on that night of November 17, 1793, rain fell, turned to sleet, and cooled the flames of Albany's first great fire.

The damage was extensive. Coupled with another flame-up the next day, the fires destroyed a number of downtown businesses, warehouses, and the residences of several old Albany families. The Gansevoorts and others relocated uptown while merchants and traders built new and larger places of business away from the old urban core that had centered on the old Dutch Reformed Church. For over a hundred years, this area had been Albany's prime commercial and residential location. Now these functions would spread out to other parts of the city and into the new production centers forming in the greater region.

Everyone knew that the fires were the work of arsonists. No

one was surprised when three slaves were arrested and charged with the crimes that the newspapers announced were punishable by death. Despite the support of a number of Albany's leading citizens, in the Spring the slave Pomp and two young black women were hanged. A large minority of African ancestry had lived in Albany since its earliest days. By the 1790s, a dozen free black households and more than five hundred slaves constituted a visible community presence whose status was evolving from slavery to freedom. Many Albany people were perplexed by this obvious minority and some were uncomfortable with the implications of their new status as free men and women.[4]

These dramatic events represent significant themes in the growth and development of the city of Albany during the latter part of the eighteenth century. This essay has introduced four incidents that occurred in Albany during the era of the Constitution as indicators of the city's coming of age. At the same time, these episodes represent symbolic bridges between this community's pioneer experience and its emergence as the modern American city destined to prosper as the "capital of the Empire State." A number of individuals played significant roles in Albany's evolution and their stories dramatize the rise of Albany as a center of government, commerce, innovation, and urban life.

By 1780, the struggle between Great Britain and its former colonies had reached an impasse. After four years of intense fighting, the war appeared to be stalemated as neither side could muster the resources or energy for a decisive campaign to bring it to a definite conclusion. Influenced by the presence of the French on the side of the Americans, the British abandoned force and decided to negotiate with the rebels. Although the peace treaty still was three years away and a major military action hit the South in 1781, overall, the combatants sought conciliatory measures at the European peace talks while avoiding major confrontations in America.

In the meantime, those living in the not-so United States sought to come to grips with pressing domestic issues and to resume the settlement and development that had been put on hold after the Boston Tea Party in 1773. At the more local level, an unprecedented wave of immigration during the decade following the end of the French and Indian War in 1763 had affected the American landscape in two general ways: One was rural, as farmers recruited in Ireland, Scotland, and Germany poured into the American backcountry and claimed the good land between the earlier settlements and the Indian territory. By 1780, these husbandmen had tamed that wilderness enough to produce a surplus of agricultural products and also had raised a new generation of pioneer farmers who joined a peer group of landless sons of New England in looking covetously at the previously forbidden lands in the West.

The second tradition was more urban and involved the destinations for farm products, the exchange of goods and services, production of finished items formerly imported from Europe, and the staging of the assault on the great American interior. After the major urban nodes of Philadelphia, New York, and Boston—and the smaller Atlantic seaport towns—a number of trade and service centers farther inland had sprung up to collect countryside produce, provide services, channel the flow of people west, and also to try their hands at nascent manufacturing. Fed by the products and nurtured by the needs of rapidly growing hinterlands, these regional entrepots of Richmond, Baltimore, Lancaster, and Albany were the prime "boom towns" of the 1780s.[5]

Located 150 miles up the Hudson River, Albany represented a bustling example of the regional center ready for its "takeoff." Geography dictated that dozens of people would pass through the Albany crossroads each day on their way to the frontier. The city's commercial, service, and hostelry resources permitted many of them to pause there for a night, a fortnight, or an annum. And the obvious opportunities to stay longer and adjust traditional activities to the new realities of independence, enlightenment, and industrialization persuaded many pioneers to end their quest at the west bank of the Hudson and to apply their talents and energies in Albany—thus taking advantage of the abundant opportunities associated with its location, economic situation, and long history. In the 1780s, newcomers from New England, the other states, and from Europe were prime movers in transforming old Albany into a service center destined to prosper in the new nation about to be created by the Industrial Revolution and the United States Constitution.[6]

But unlike its more adolescent counterparts, already-old Albany had a well-established identity of its own. Chartered as a city in 1686, Albany was able to enhance its position as a regional service center, transportation interchange, and seat of power long after the passing of the fur trade and the frontier. Albany's evolution hinged on the ability of its leading citizens to adapt the community's functions through their own enterprises to new political and economic conditions and to structure the activities of Albany's more ordinary people in a range of patron-client relationships, which were based partially on kinship and which often reached several generations into the community's past. Historically, Albany's leaders, to their benefit, had been able to reconcile world events and other larger issues with local realities. In the 1780s, most of the progressive leaders (a mix of native sons and ambitious newcomers) understood that the enabling provisions of the Federal Constitution represented a new opportunity that could be used to their advantage and to Albany's benefit.

But a community as old as any in the United States and one with commercial and service heritages still derivative of its earliest incarnations was bound to be wedded to its past and to its time-tested traditions. This was particularly evident in its people. Many of Albany's 3,000 residents traced their ancestry to the first days of community life thus stamping Albany society with an unmistakable character of continuity. In 1780, Albany's wealthiest man was General Philip Schuyler, a descendant of a Dutch woodcarver who became the community's foremost figure a century before. Albany's favorite son was college-educated Stephen Van Rensselaer—twenty-one years old in 1784 and the last of the "patroons." Detached from city politics and business, the Schuyler and Van Rensselaer presence transcended the city limits and sometimes gave them the appearance of being Albany's absentee owners.[7]

The largest Albany family of the 1780s, the Lansings, counted more than fifteen households in the city. Their continued success mirrored the coming of age of the three sons of the original émigrés of a hundred years earlier and was characterized by the family's ability to adapt to new realities which in the 1680s took them from fur trading to baking and butchering, and in the 1780s from serving local customers to providing a range of services to government, transient, and professional clients. By the 1780s, the family's representation across the community's socio-economic spectrum ranged from "Chancellor" John Lansing, Jr., a delegate to the Philadelphia convention and mayor of Albany from 1786 to 1790, through a number of successful and long-lived merchants and shippers to Sanders Lansing, the city's best baker. Beyond the name, the Lansings also were the most typical of old Albany families as a number of their daughters tied the community together with marriages into every other major city family.[8]

Traditional names such as Bleecker, Bradt, Douw, Fonda, Gansevoort, Hansen, Roseboom, Van Deusen, Van Heusen, Van Schaick, Visscher, and Wendell (legatees of the original Dutch founders now in their fourth and fifth generations in America) still stood out on Albany rolls. Prominent too were the descendents of the post-New Netherland settlers, an ethically diverse group that included Beekmans, Bogarts, Brookses, Coopers, De Garmos, Hewsons, Hiltons, Hogans, Maases (Bloomendal), Pruyns, Radcliffs, Ten Eycks, Winnes, Yateses, and a number of other families. Like most colonial in-migrants, these newcomers married local women, raised large families, and over the preceding century, managed to make a place in the community. On the other hand, another old Albany name disappeared from the city records each year, as oldliners died or moved out—because they were unable to change or because they had become too uncomfortable with the pace and practices of the new order.[9]

Their places were more than taken by immigrants. Those from New England brought wives with them, moved into the vacant buildings, and launched the printing, banking, and development enterprises that characterized the community into the twentieth century. These newcomers did not seem to mind that no Congregational meeting-house would be established until the 1800s. Instead, they applied themselves to more temporal pursuits and, during the 1780s, began to transform the Albany economy. These puritans had become "Yankees." Some New Englanders managed to invest success in a son, while the other offspring typically found their fortunes beyond Albany.[10]

More heterogeneous than the Yankees were other American migrants from New York City, the lower Hudson Valley, New Jersey, Pennsylvania, and the South. These newcomers found immediate success in Albany because they came with skills that were very marketable in the boom economy. Some were inclined toward business; others brought with them manufacturing skills or lines of credit that reached beyond New York to Philadelphia, Boston, and even to Europe. The well-educated had been recruited as teachers and attorneys and quickly found warm places with developing government business in the new state capital. The success stories of Stephen Lush of New York and King's College; Dutchess-born Egbert Benson, also of King's College; Princeton graduates John Bay of Maryland, Peter Elmendorf and George Merchant, both of New Jersey; and John Lovett of Yale stand as prime examples. Physicians, including Samuel Stringer of Maryland, Hunloke Woodruff of New Jersey, Wilhelmus Mancius from Kingston, and a dozen other medical men at the wartime hospital made Albany a nucleus of medical knowledge. Those who remained, established Albany as a health care center in the years to come. The sons of these doctors and lawyers became Albany's professionals and included artists, authors, scientists, and inventors a generation later.[11]

Others had recently relocated from New York City. They were refugees and opportunists. This upriver migration began over a century earlier with the arrival of Beekmans, Cuylers, Ten Eycks, and others. It continued on a modest scale throughout the colonial period with the Bloodgoods of Long Island, the De Peyster and Waters families, and a number of individual migrants such as John Tayler—soon to be lieutenant-governor—and John Roorbach, schoolteacher of German ancestry. And it had escalated since the outbreak of the war as more than a tenth of Albany's people were refugees. Fleeing from the British, they found Albany a less perilous place to conduct their business temporarily, and they joined the others in orchestrating Albany's boom. The war brought the families of Gerardus De Peyster, Evert Bancker, Morgan Lewis, Nicholas Roosevelt and others to Albany. These advantaged New Yorkers quickly found profitable opportunities in upriver business and in the activities of the new state government. Most of them returned home after 1783 having forged political connections and business relationships with Albany people that held promise for the future.[12]

A large general group came directly from Europe. Represented chiefly by the Sanders, Glen, and Livingston families before the 1750s, Scottish Calvinists constituted a major immigrant group to Albany from the 1750s until the outbreak of hostilities in 1775. With more than fifty new households in the city, many of these emigres were business people who traded in finished items, married the daughters of local families, and supported the formation of a Presbyterian meeting house. The Henrys, McClallens, and Shipboys were able to stay in the community because they joined with the revolutionaries while many of their countrymen were forced out of New York because they were unwilling to fight against the king. Scottish and Scots-Irish immigration resumed its high pitch with the coming of peace. While some of these emigres made a major impact on Albany business, a larger number of the sons of Scotland settled into the more working-class lives of the artisan and the laborer.[13]

By the 1780s, the descendants of garrison soldiers of Irish background, like the Barrets, Hewsons, Hogans, and Williamses, were well-established in Albany's service industries, had become Episcopalians, and seemed to have little in common with their more recently arrived countrymen, who were Roman Catholics and were best able to sell their services as laborers. These Irish newcomers joined with Albany's small enclave of French-descended businessmen and shopkeepers to found St. Mary's Catholic Church in 1797.[14]

Paralleling Albany's old and new Irish and French were émigrés from Germany who found little comfort in the fact that many of the descendants of Albany's New Netherland-era settlers were also of German background. The Ten Broecks, Gansevoorts, Hallenbecks and Witbecks had long since become acculturated —acculturation having been a requisite for success. Without connections, and distinguished by language barriers, Albany's recent German émigrés, the Abels, Heyers, Hoghstrassers, and Rubys, came together with local farmers in the traditional South Pearl Street Lutheran Church and the newly-formed German Reformed church in North Albany, and seized on the need for overland transportation and food processing to carve their niche in the city's service economy.[15]

One in ten of the community's people was of African ancestry. Until the 1780s, almost all of these early Albanians were slaves. Held by merchants, artisans, and shippers, African-Americans were found in many city households and were the backbone of Albany's commercial, service, and domestic workforce. The census of 1790 counted 572 slaves but also identified twenty-six individuals in seven households as "free people of color." These African-Americans practiced the same manual and service occupations as their bonded counterparts, but only they worked for wages, purchased houselots, married, raised families, and sought a better life on their own. In-migration and emancipation would swell the number of free people of color to over 500 by 1810 and would eliminate Albany's slave population by the 1820s.

During the era of the Constitution, Albany's large slave population (14 percent of the city total) was becoming unwieldly. Most of the community's slaveowners understood that slavery soon would pass and that paid labor represented the workforce of the future. With the ideal of freedom a reality, slaves grew anxious for a new life. Albany bondsmen were able to pry from their owners concessions that ranged from control over increasing portions of their time to promises of emancipation in the future. Except for those who had not found substitutes for slave labor, most owners were resigned to nominal control over their human property and seem to have accepted slave marriages and the birth of children as part of the traditional rights of family life.

As "part-time" slaves and free blacks began to compete for laborer and service jobs with the young, the newly arrived, and the poor, their presence began to intrude upon those white workers who also sought employment as wage laborers. While the wealthy and Albany's elite aritsans could afford to support emancipation for both altruistic and economic reasons (the creation of a new group of clients), ordinary people did not look forward to competing with former slaves for jobs or to supporting them if they became impoverished. Freedom for blacks conjured up a number of potential problems that created some uneasiness among the less affluent. These tensions surfaced in a number of curious ways of which the aftermath of the great fire represented a particularly graphic example.[16]

By the end of the War for Independence, women as heads of households had become a permanent feature of Albany society. Widowed heads of households dated to the seventeenth century, accounting for 10 to 20 percent of the city's householders. In Albany's early days, widowhood was brief; most women remarried quickly, and permanent widows typically were elderly. By the 1700s, husbands often adopted the practice of bequeathing wives the use of the family estate as long as they did not remarry, thus making their continued widowhood an economic asset in that widows were able to control property while married, and re-married women could not. During the eighteenth-century, the tendency for widows not to remarry continued to increase, regardless of their age, which gave Albany a growing number of households headed by widows, who often survived by renting business space, taking in boarders, and sometimes even continuing the business and craft activities of their late husbands.

After mid-century, the population of women as permanent heads of households received an additional boost as a number of daughters of Albany families inherited city houses and chose to live there unmarried, often with women relatives, for long spinsterhoods. Mary Van Schaick, Margaret Hun, Jane Van Vechten, Rachel De Garmo, and the Douw sisters, Catherine and Rachel, who lived in their inherited family house from the 1770s to Catherine's death in 1806, were prominent independent women of the post-Revolutionary era.[17]

A final major element of the Albany demographic mosaic were the hundreds of people who were visible in the city on any given day but who were not reflected in census schedules, lists of members and participants, or rolls of owners. These were people in motion—the transients. In addition to being the principal population center north of New York City, during the 1780s Albany was one of the major interchanges in the new United States. Albany's historic role as a crossroads was the result of its superb location at the head of navigation of the Hudson, the most efficient portage to the Mohawk, and at the junction of a number of already established overland routes. The success of this ideally situated entrepot was rooted in Albany's long history as a service center: a convenient and hospitable place where regional husbandmen brought animal, farm, and forest products for sale and found supplies, service, and safety; a way station where new settlers switched modes of transportation, replenished supplies, and then were funnelled to dates with destiny elsewhere; and, especially after the war, a place where lumber, grain, and livestock from Albany's hinterland and the frontier were consolidated, processed, and then shipped out.

These crossroads activities had sustained the Albany economy for years. At the same time, they gave the city a bulging presence as it overflowed with people from elsewhere, who were in town for a special event or activity or on their way to some place else. No longer at the edge of the frontier, post-war Albany hosted thousands of American pioneers. Even before the end of hostilities in 1783, every day was market day as country people mingled with those from New England, from the other middle states, and with immigrants from Europe who had paused on their odysseys to new homes in the west. Buying and selling became so pervasive that a "market house" was erected in the middle of "Market Street" and a number of "market places" began to appear on city maps and in literary accounts. Business people set up stores and storehouses, petitioned the city corporation to improve the Albany waterfront and transportation links with the interior, and called on mayors John J. Beekman and John Lansing as "clerk of the market" to set standard weights and business practices.[18] The decision to locate the market house in the street was in contrast to the movement whereby street-centered churches were relocated to make way for trade.

While a new day was dawning for business, the first and most profound impetus for growth and change came from one of Albany's early catalysts—the business of government. The old English fort was gone, and the city government had settled into evolved manifestations of its traditional functions minus Indian diplomacy, but the economy received an immediate boost from the prospects of supporting the business of New York State —Albany's first great service industry since the fur trade.

After the legislative session of 1780, the state government moved downriver to Poughkeepsie, Kingston, and, after the war, to New York City before returning to Albany late in 1788. Although legislators were meeting elsewhere, government agencies and agents, ranging from land commissioners to the state surveyor, found Albany an appropriate headquarters. By the late 1780s, both state and county courts, registry and regulatory agencies, and a number of fledgling government departments, including the new board of regents, were located in Albany. Their activities attracted administrators and attorneys. Many of these newcomers were well educated and brought with them professional and business contacts that further advertized Albany's resources and virtues.

Those involved in and interested in the decisions to be made by state government competed for business space on the city's main streets with elite merchants, public house owners, entrepreneurs, and lawyers. Most of these interested parties were newcomers like Stephen Lush, a learned attorney, exchanged prisoner of war, and Governor Clinton's secretary. Lush married Dr. Samuel Stringer's daughter, shared living space in Stringer's grand new home on North Market Street, and, with the help of his brother Richard, amassed a fortune speculating on military land bounties and government notes.[19]

With the end of the war, the central business began to be built over. Many of the architectural legacies of New Netherland were replaced first by larger Georgian homes, whose broad sides faced the street, and by Federal-style stores and offices, larger business buildings that could accommodate a number of sales people, clerks, and accountants. The old brick townhouses, such as the landmark homes of Abraham Wendell, Balthazar Lydius, and Jacob Vanderheyden, became more and more conspicuous as their comparatively miniature proportions contrasted with the significantly larger structures of the new city. The transitional character of the "downtown" Albany of the post-Revolutionary period is represented in the reminiscent drawings of James Eights.[20]

Squeezed out of the old urban core, where coopers once lived next to council members, a great number of occupations—lesser shop keepers, artisans, tinkers, tradesmen, and resource processors (tapsters, tanners, and timbermen) and a growing group of wage-earners who formed the city's rank-and-file workforce—spread north and south into the fields formerly occupied only by the mansions of the Van Rensselaers and Schuylers. As early as the 1760s, these lands beyond the central city area had been gridded and were defined by streets named for animals, birds, and notable personages. Ravine areas along Foxes Creek were developed to become Fox Street—the address of a number of workers, including those at Gerrit Witbeck's new nail manufactory. The "Gallows Hill" area, known as "the Plain," was serviced by Plain Street and permitted development of the high ground between the Ruttenkill and Beaverkill. "Arbor Hill," along the city's northern boundary, was divided and marketed; and wetlands along the river were divided into houselots on newly created streets and sold to younger sons of city families and to newcomers. Their modest homes in the North and South ends stood in contrast to the grand mansions and stately town houses of leading merchants, financiers, and professional people.

Since the end of the war, the rough road leading up the hill toward Schenectady and the West became well-trodden and was dotted with buildings. Called Lion Street (now Washington Avenue), this sandy thoroughfare marked development that extended past Swan Street near a site where a number of recently arrived Scots were running an inn, stables, and general store known as "Mc Donald's." Expansion continued west along this route as other "halfway houses" sprang up on the "King's Highway" and on the other roads out of Albany as wagon and coach transportation became widespread for the first time. Residential development filled in the newly divided houselots as the city side of these roads became streets. Always an outstanding community feature, stables numbered almost 200 in the city by 1800, as the requirements of coach, draught, and farm animals created an important service industry.

Business people, tradesmen, and transporters also set up on river-level Market Street in a variety of new structures all the way north to the manor house of Stephen Van Rensselaer, about a mile north of the Dutch Church. Multi-storied and generous in floor space, many of the new buildings were large enough to serve as offices and stores as well as residences for the owners and a number of lodgers. During the latter stages of the war, Albany had begun to accommodate an increasing number of unattached workers, vendors, officials, and lobbyists in dwellings large enough to be called boarding houses. Evolving out of inns run by a widow, a failed merchant, or an enterprising newcomer, a number of roominghouses and large downtown hotels had emerged by the end of the century.

The former cow path from State Street to the south pastures became Washington Street (then South Pearl Street) and ran past the Yates and Schuyler mansions all the way to the Van Rensselaers' "Cherry Hill"—elegant counterpoints to the large number of newly built, frame homes of the city's marginal makers, fixers, teamsters, and wage earners. The first residents of the subdivided pasture lots (mostly on the streets crossing Washington Street) were a mixed group of ordinary people including sons of established families, migrants and immigrants, and also a number of African-American householders.

The buildings on the older avenues and alleys crossing State,

Market, and Pearl Streets were renovated or rebuilt to accommodate multi-use occupancy. These were the homes and shops of more comfortable artisans and tradesmen and of widows who were sometimes able to derive additional income by renting space to tenants and boarders.

Despite increased new building in the city during the 1780s, housing, shop, and business space was in short supply, especially on the terms required to serve an elevated volume and accelerated pace of activity. Until the older Dutch-style dwellings of the old Albany were replaced by larger, more urban public and business buildings (many of which would be designed by Ezra Ames, Albany's first architect after 1800), existing city structures were forced to accommodate a number of uses. Few downtown buildings remained purely residential or single-purpose places of business.

By the mid-1780s, Albany had outgrown its colonial confines, a problem that was only temporarily eased by the removal of the stockade a decade earlier. Public buildings like the city hall also served as a state house, court house, and jail. Each of the city's six churches and the majority of the taverns and inns also served as community centers hosting meetings, itinerant preachers, and other public events. Even the city's fire pumper was stored in a shed behind St. Peter's Episcopal Church. By the 1790s, Albany was in desperate need of more urban buildings to accommodate its burgeoning enterprises and bulging population.

As the State/Pearl/Market Street urban spine became more exclusively office, business, and elite residence, and the buildings crowded together on the cross streets became a mixture of homes and small shops, major production activities were shifted exclusively to the edges of the city. Brewing and distilling, tanning operations, smithies and larger metal shops, woodworking trades and adjacent lumber yards, brickyards, and Albany's first factories began to appear during the 1780s north of the city limits along the river and in the South End on the new streets formerly known as the city pastures. These "manufactories" and the distilleries, and lumber and brickyards as well, were able to produce in volume because their proprietors were able to employ a number of workers from among the new labor pool of younger sons and immigrants.

The Hudson River had been Albany's lifeline since its earliest days. Until the third quarter of the century, however, Albany's waterfront facilities had been primitive. Shipping was at the mercy of the current, as the shoreline was eroded and then silted in by tidal and flood deposition. After the last colonial war, which ended in 1763, the city corporation sponsored construction of Albany's first permanent docks. Three wharves at the ends of major cross streets represented a dramatic improvement of shipping facilities. Over the next two decades, the city further improved the waterfront by building a seawall and quay, which allowed sloops and larger vessels to be moored dockside instead of being anchored in deep water and serviced by tenders. Commercial space on the city docks and along the quay was leased to business people and transporters, which gave the waterfront a bustling market-like appearance for the first time. Quay Street (on the river) and Dock Street (parallel to and a block inland of Quay Street) were defined quickly after the end of the Revolutionary War by the store/homes of shippers and shopkeepers. Quayside quickly became overcrowded as floods of farm and forest products from the hinterland and new frontier areas were stacked up on any available lots and even cluttered the roads to the water while awaiting export. At the same time, manufactured items and the belongings of pioneers heading west competed for storage space with grain, barrelled beverages, and lumber. Overflow goods and materials were placed in warehouses and yards north and south of the port area, while shops and taverns appeared on the cross streets that connected the market and the river. Before the end of the century, the water level area south of State Street had become a lodging-house section with a number of large hotels under construction south of city hall along South Market Street.[21]

An "Albany Fleet" of sloops which traditionally enjoyed a lion's share of the Hudson River carrying trade and gave the community a nautical flavor, kept pace with Albany's maturing business and service enterprises during the postwar years. Composed of more than a hundred locally-built schooners, sloops, smaller craft, and the ferries which linked Albany and Greenbush, these small boats jammed the Albany port area as they carried cargoes and passengers and connected all of the communities in the Hudson drainage basin.

Many Albany boys grew up with some experience as crewmen, watermen, or dockworkers. During colonial days, most of these young workers gave up sailing and waterfront activities when they started their own families. Others continued to sail—as skippers of the sloops of city merchants, as pilots, or as captains of their own small boats—although often on a part-time basis. As Albany became the home port of a large number of watercraft that increasingly jammed the riverfront, the city government built more docking space and began to rent space along the quay.

Few Albany boys had become career sailors or dockmen during the colonial period. Wartime needs extended the sailing days of many community men, who were invaluable in moving soldiers and supplies up and down the valley. Since the 1770s, however, the number of adult sailors and particularly of support workers (longshoremen and watermen) on the waterfront had increased markedly. Water-based jobs employed newcomers, free blacks, and also the younger sons of Albany families, who previously would have left the community to become tenant farmers. Albany was developing an enclave of maritime workers that included ocean-going skippers like Stewart Dean, who regularly visited Atlantic coastal ports all the way to the West Indies; sailors who manned these schooners and sloops; dockhands; and a supporting cast of sail and rope makers, shipwrights, and naval products processors.[22]

By the 1780s, new physical facilities enabled Albany to become a major river port. Its location at the nexus point in the flow of goods, products, and settlers in major proportions brought a vitality to the city beyond anything known in the past. No longer the last stop, Albany instead served as a transformer or transfer point between the Euro-Atlantic civilization of the seaboard states and the untamed bounty of the new West. By the end of the war, the Albany Post Road connected Albany and New York by stagecoach. The improvement of this east bank route during the 1780s caused the city fathers to authorize new ferries at the north and south ends of the city to provide more efficient access. Before the end of the century, improved roads extended out from city streets and became highways into the interior—the Great Western Turnpike, the Delaware Turnpike, and a half-dozen others. A number of city families began to be identified as teamsters and competed for the business of moving freight inland from the river. Carts, wagons, sleighs, and later coaches were built in Albany shops that began to employ numbers of people in an enterprise that required the skills of those who worked in wood, metal, and leather.[23]

While numerous and diverse, colonial Albany's industrial activities had been small in scale—typically a craftsman assisted by family members, by a slave, or by a single paid helper. Although Albany crafts produced a volume of leather goods, kegs, and other wood products, little remained for merchandizing externally. Albany's smiths and tailors spent most of their time filling local orders to make and mend household artifacts and to produce necessary metal and cloth items, which left them little opportunity to produce and stock a line of products. Bricks, tiles, and wooden building materials were made locally but those too were consumed by local demand. Under the British, production for export had been prohibited. After American independence removed that restriction, a market economy for surplus products first became legitimate. After the war, producers and investors came together in Albany to meet a widespread demand for finished items that formerly were in short supply and mostly were imported from Europe.[24]

By the mid 1780s, a few production centers had appeared in the city. In contrast to older and simpler craft shops, they were able to manufacture larger quantities of items for sale because they employed numbers of workers who turned out products in volume. Gerrit Witbeck opened a factory on Foxes Creek in 1787 that cut and finished nails. His enterprise attracted the attention of three local businessmen who financed another nail factory later that year. A soap and candle factory opened in 1788, inspired by the wartime successes of James Caldwell, a recently arrived promoter from northern Ireland.[25] Caldwell can be called the father of Albany manufacturing. By the end of the war, he had turned from candle and soap making and the milling of mustard seeds to a cooperative glass manufacturing enterprise and then to the processing and marketing of tobacco and chocolate products. These endeavors were made possible by Caldwell's understanding of general manufacturing principles, his ability to involve investors (and even to secure public funding), and chiefly by his success in attracting and managing factory workers. Caldwell advertised for apprentices, helpers, and workers in the press and particularly favored the new labor pool of recent European émigrés. At one time, he employed as many as fifty workers.

Successful in Albany business since the 1770s, Caldwell and entrepreneurs like him made few friends among long-time residents of the city. Able to remain above suspicion himself, during the war Caldwell had come forward as bailsman for a number of fellow Scots arrested for anti-Patriot activities. Supplying soap, candles, and other items to the Revolutionary governments and armies, he became wealthy in a wartime economy that brought hard times to many Albany households. With profits to lend, he listed many Albany people, and the city government as well, in his extensive ledger of credit clients. Partners and beneficiaries in his business ventures, however, were exclusively relative newcomers—opportunists such as Robert Mc Clallen, John Maley, and Christopher Batterman. Coupled with Caldwell's preference for European-born workers, traditional Albany people came to resent the prosperity that rewarded the dramatic alterations taking place in the city as a result of the investments and innovations made by Caldwell and others like him. The brick that felled this aggressive and prominent entrepreneur in 1787 as he paraded alongside fellow future captains of industry may not have been simply an errant missile. Formerly comfortable city workers understandably could be offended by those who offered better opportunities in a factory or workhouse and who preferred Europeans and the sons of New England as employees while they began to feel the decline of their own living standard.[26]

On one level, the Albany ratification parade seemed to celebrate the vitality of the city's production economy, with every traditional craft and trade represented by a contingent of ebullient artisans, who looked forward to profits from new market opportunities that would be created and protected by the government to be established under the United States Constitution. The mottos underscoring their individual coat of arms, however, reveal a more fated foreboding of the future. While the cartmen's epigram prayed "We hope to rest in God" and the masons proclaimed "Our trust is in God," the manufacturers and merchants placed a more optimistic and material faith in the future, exhorting "Success to American Manufacturers" and "May our exports exceed our imports." While independent crafts and trades would remain fixtures of the city's production economy, the number of wage workers surpassed them within two decades.

The recently-arrived with new and more sophisticated production skills prospered while the traditional trades practiced by the Albany shoemaker, the cooper, and the smith continued to lose ground and passed from a number of long-time city families within a single generation. Many sons of trades families had taken dramatic career turns, to work for someone else in a factory, in freighting, for general wages, or most frequently to leave the city entirely. Those who remained, to fashion and fix clothing, boats, and implements as their fathers did in days past, found that their products and services were becoming less and less competitive.[27]

Spearheaded by newcomers from New England and Europe, a new spirit of enterprise and innovation had taken hold in Albany by the 1790s, to guide the community through its first period of transformation. Each year, the common council included another member who was not an Albany native. The new city fathers began to implement internal changes that addressed the needs of a multiplying urban population in what was becoming a modern, commercial city. The infrastructural improvements noted earlier had given Albany a port, a network of roads into the interior, and a number of new buildings. These would be expanded greatly and would provide the setting for Albany's growth in the immediate future. During the mayoral terms of Abraham Yates, Jr. (1790–96) and Abraham Ten Broeck (1796–98)—venerable revolutionaries and representatives of a passing generation of old-style popular and aristocratic leaders —an emerging progressive city council turned to practical issues such as street paving and lighting, water and waste control, fire and police protection, the regulation of business activities through comprehensive licensing and leasing, poor relief, and the explosive development of the mile-long riverside district for commercial use, which transformed Albany into a great inland riverport long before the opening of the Erie Canal.[28]

During the 1790s, a mixed group of native-born and newly arrived investors came together to establish a merchant's exchange, which led to the city's first banks, a number of incorporated businesses, and other chartered development ventures including stage lines, turnpikes, and canal companies. This group of about a hundred men also were founders of Albany's schools, its library, other community organizations, and also of Schenectady-based Union College. They were Albany's civic-minded. Their interests would be best served if development was ordered by laws and bylaws and structured by social organizations that brought community people together for mutually beneficial activities.[29]

The proliferation of enterprise in post-war Albany affected every part of the city's population. These developments made public a polarization in the distribution of Albany's wealth that had begun right after the decline of the fur trade a hundred years earlier. By the end of the eighteenth century, a relatively small group of developers/investors/proprietors had taken open control of the city's economic, social, and political life. These pillars of the community included some members of the city's colonial elite from the Van Rensselaer, Bleecker, Douw, Ten Eyck, Van Schaick, and Ten Broeck families. But by the early 1800s, Albany's new leadership was more accurately characterized by those who were not Albany natives. At the other end of the spectrum, a relatively large number of city residents became employees, working for wages or performing services for fees. Unlike colonial times, when workers were scarce and in demand, the terms of employment for post-Revolutionary workers were increasingly determined by the proprietors. This worker group included a large number of old family members as well as some names that had been absent from Albany rolls for almost a century. But those of native stock were leaving the city, as more flexible immigrants, migrants, and newly freed African-Americans more than took their places as members of the Albany work force.

Squeezed out during Albany's transformation were many of the smiths, shoemakers, and textile craftsmen mainline artisans who formerly earned a comfortable living making, repairing, and selling their wares. As industrious proprietors moved to concentrate production of metal, cloth, wood, and animal products in factories, these craftsmen found it more and more difficult to compete with manufactured items. A few were able to adapt their production skills to evolved crafted items like clocks and carriages, but the majority of them slipped down to working for wages while others either left the city or else entered an unrelated new line of work. A generation earlier, they had been the backbone, heart, and soul of the city's work force. By the end of the eighteenth century, Albany's traditional artisans had lost their middling places in the new industrial and service society that characterized their city in the 1800s. Finding themselves sliding farther down the economic pyramid and not positioned to benefit from any of the new investment opportunities, this group would be most opposed to progressive changes that only began with the ratification of the Federal Constitution. Freedom for slaves would add yet another competitor for the residual benefits that the city's growing worker population hoped to obtain.

By the close of the eighteenth century, the old Albany had passed. Before long, most people's recollections of it would be inspired chiefly by published reminiscences and knickerbocker histories. One by one, the visible reminders were erased. Gone were the fur traders, the fort, the stockade, and within a few years, the downtown Dutch Church. Gone too were most of the gable-faced brick townhouses of the families whose forebears had founded the community a century and a half earlier and who had been major contributors to the development of an Albany identity during the colonial era.

The 1780s represented a time of transition. Albany's economic, social, and political character changed dramatically after the end of the War for Independence. An adolescent about to come of age when Revolution removed restrictions on trade and on the development of the West, during the era of the Constitution Albany became more of a young adult. Its people underwent a crash course in the urbanizing experience while gaining its first perspectives on what the city would become in its third century. Service and information center, financial headquarters, commercial entrepot, and the capital of the new leader among the American states, Albany—with its new municipal buildings and state capitol, downtown business and commercial houses, large retail stores, riverfront basin and formal dockage, warehousing facilities, and new residential neighborhoods sprawling beyond a too-small city limits—was ready for a new future.

Notes

The writing of this article was made possible by the interest, energy, and general commitment of the current and past Associates, interns, staff members, and other supporters of the Colonial Albany Social History Project. Since 1981 more than a hundred individuals have joined together in a cooperative effort dedicated to recovering the life stories of all of those who lived in the city of Albany before 1800, to placing their lives in a community context, and to presenting their stories to a range of audience groups in ways that are both relevant and accessible to diverse interests and abilities.

In this effort, special acknowledgement is due to my associates Jan Ghee, Glenn Griffith, and Joyce Patterson. I also appreciate the generous support of George Damiano and Leonard Tantillo.

1. George Clinton described the weather and other situations in letters to William Floyd and Robert R. Livingston in January 1780, *Public Papers of George Clinton, First Governor of New York* (Albany, 1901), 5:443–48. Legislative sessions are outlined in *Civil List and Constitutional History of the Colony and State of New York*, compiled by Edgar A. Werner (Albany, 1889), 371–73, 409–15. General community information presented throughout this article has been gathered by the members of the Colonial Albany Social History Project since 1982 and has been applied toward the development of a detailed, lifecourse biography for every person who lived in the city of Albany and who was born before the end of 1800. This resource material and the plan for conducting research are described in detail in "The People of Colonial Albany: A Community History Project," a comprehensive guide to the research, programming, and service activities of the Colonial Albany Project. The "Guide" has been revised and issued annually since 1984. The 1989 edition is available from the CAP office, 3093 Cultural Education Center, Albany, N.Y. 12230. Each of the 16,000 lifecourse biographies now in progress is fully documented. These are referred to throughout by parenthetical computer database numbers. Particularly helpful for the chronology of the early 1780s is Don R. Gerlach, *Proud Patriot: Philip Schuyler and the War of Independence, 1775–1783* (Syracuse, 1987).

2. The most comprehensive information about the *Experiment* and its voyage is found in William J. Wilgus, *The Life of Captain Stewart Dean: A Character of the American Revolution* (Ascutney, Vt., 1942). For Dean, see Colonial Albany Social History Project lifecourse biography case number 7800 and the sources cited therein. For the Albany fleet, see for example Patrick M'Robert, *A Tour Through Part of the North Provinces of America, 1774–1775* (Edinburg, Scotland, 1776), 7–9.

3. The ratification celebration was described in the *Albany Gazette* of August 28, 1788. See also "Celebration of the Adoption of the Constitution," *Annals of Albany,* compiled by Joel Munsell (Albany, 1850), 1:330–335.

4. Newspaper accounts of the fire are summarized as "Notes from the Newspapers," in Munsell, *Annals of Albany,* 3:160–61. See also "The Conflagration of 1793," in Joel Munsell, *Collections on the History of Albany* (Albany, 1867), 2:378–82. For a more focused and slightly different summary of the incident, see Alice P. Kenney, *The Gansevoorts of Albany: Dutch Patricians in the Upper Hudson Valley* (Syracuse, 1969), 135–36.

5. We still lack a comprehensive study of New York society during the latter stages of the war for Independence, as each of the major treatments are either one-dimensional in scope or else overburdened by a theoretical framework. However, this section must acknowledge the contributions of Edward Countryman most impressively made in *A People in Revolution: The American Revolution and Political Society in New York, 1760–1790* (Baltimore, 1981; New York, 1989). This volume was recently published in paperback by W. W. Norton with the assistance of the New York State Bicentennial Commission. For the settlement of the American backcountry, see D. W. Meinig, *The Shaping of America: A Geographical Perspective on 500 Years of History, Volume I: Atlantic*

America, 1492–1800 (New Haven, 1987), a particularly enlightening synthesis of the settlement story.

6. Between the 1760s and 1790, the city's population showed almost no absolute increase—holding at about 3,000, as hundreds of newcomers just about replaced outmigrants. But between 1790 and 1820 the number of people living in Albany increased fourfold to almost 13,000. With natural increase and mortality fairly constant during this period, this fourfold increase is attributable largely to immigration. Early Albany demography and immigration history are considered in Stefan Bielinski, "The People of Colonial Albany, 1650–1800: The Profile of a Community," *Authority and Resistance in Early New York*, edited by William Pencak and Conrad E. Wright (New York, 1988), 1–26. People leaving is the subject of Bielinski, "Coming and Going in Early America: The People of Colonial Albany and Outmigration," *De Halve Maen* 60 (October 1987), 12–18.

7. Both of Don R. Gerlach's authoritative volumes on Philip Schuyler portray him as aloof from civic affairs although, in terms of wealth and influence, he certainly was Albany's foremost personage. See his *Philip Schuyler and the American Revolution in New York, 1733–1777* (Lincoln, Neb., 1964) and *Proud Patriot: Philip Schuyler and the War of Independence, 1775–1783*. For a comprehensive evaluation of Schuyler's Albany-based career, see CAP biography (1750). Like Schuyler an Albany property-holder, Stephen Van Rensselaer (1764–1839) (case 5115) lived in an elegant mansion located north of the city. Also like the general, he was a major contributor to community improvement enterprises throughout his long life. Yet he too avoided direct involvement in the workings of city government and business. These functions passed to his cousin and nephew, Jeremiah Van Rensselaer (5085) and Philip S. Van Rensselaer (5106). Philip Schuyler, however, had no city-based surrogates. By the 1780s, the Schuyler family network had lost its once-compelling power base as only two Schuyler households were described on the 1790 census of the city.

8. The largest and most complex of the early Albany family groups, the Lansings lack a modern family history comparable to those published during the 1980s on the Schuylers, Quackenbushes, Oothouts, and others. Materials relating to these and other early Albany families are chronicled in *Sources on the People of Colonial Albany: Family Histories and Genealogies*, compiled by Anne La Falce and Linda Keller (Albany, 1989). For the Lansings, see Claude G. Munsell, *The Lansing Family: A Genealogy of the Descendents of Gerrit Fredrickse Lansing who came to America from Hassel, Province of Overijssel, Holland in 1640* (privately printed, 1916). For John Lansing, Jr. (1754–1829), one of fifty "Johannes Lansings" in the Colonial Albany Project community population, see (3755). Long-lived contemporaries included John Jo. Lansing (3743), John E. Lansings (3751), and John A. Lansing (3754). For Sanders Lansing (1723–1807), see (3756).

9. The first chapter of the saga of Albany's children of New Netherland is Stefan Bielinski et al, "What Became of the New Netherland Dutch? Settling In and Spreading Out in Colonial Albany," an analysis of the origins of the city's population at the time of the census of 1697. This article is forthcoming in a volume on the history of the family from Duquesne University Press. The profile of Albany society during the latter half of the eighteenth century is derived from a comparative analysis of census, assessment rolls, and other community-based survey documents.

10. Artisans and shopkeepers from New England began to trickle into Albany during the 1750s. Comprising printers, hatters, watchmakers, and other tinkerers, their in-migration accelerated during the 1760s and again during the War for Independence, which brought the families of Elisha Crane (7713), Edward Cump-

ston (7684), James Gray (8256), and others to Albany as permanent residents. Migration accelerated during the 1780s and continued in force until after the end of the War of 1812. By the 1790s, these Yankees had become a significant minority group and a major element of the city's business and commerce, and of its education and professional establishment. Elisha Jenkins (3880), whose family was distinguished in Albany's millinery work, was the first New Englander appointed mayor in 1816. Yankee contributions to the transformation are chronicled in Jonathan Tenney, *New England in Albany* (Boston, 1883).

11. See CAP biographical case files for John Bay (7284), a teacher; Dr. William Bay (7285), one of the founders of the Albany Medical Society; teachers Peter Elmendorf (7945), George Merchant (1021), Egbert Benson (7321), and John Lovett (3891). The son of an Annapolis physician, Samuel Stringer (5046), was a leader of the Albany revolutionary movement and a prominent advocate of vaccination for smallpox. For Wilhelmus Mancius, see 6628; for Hunloke Woodruff, see 3524. Foremost among Albany's famous sons was scientist and inventor Joseph Henry (8420), who started out as a teacher at the Albany Academy. Another notable example was the artist and scientist, James Eights—a physician's son. See Char Miller and Naomi Goldsmith, "James Eights, Albany Naturalist; New Evidence," *New York History* 61 (January 1980), 23–42.

12. The seventeenth-century migration to Albany is discussed in Bielinski, "What Became of the New Netherland Dutch?" For later New York City migrants, see the biographical case files of John Tayler (1383); John Roorbach (7956); Gerardus De Peyster (7827); Evert Bancker (237); Morgan Lewis (3898); and Nicholas Roosevelt (3913). Aaron Burr and Alexander Hamilton were most notable among a number of downriver attorneys who found fortune in Albany during the latter part of the war.

13. Scots and Scots-Irish are defined here as non-Catholics. The Catholics are categorized as Irish. The Livingstons and other Scots who entered before the mid-eighteenth century, generally acculturated well, often joining the Dutch Reformed Church. Those who settled in Albany after 1750 were more ethnically distinct. See the case files for Robert Henry (8425) and his sons, Robert Mc Clallen (725) and Thomas Shipboy (5686). John Macomb (1059), a Belfast merchant who followed the British army to Albany during the 1750s and supplied the needs of its officers, is the subject of a close study of the dynamics of wartime profiteering by Joseph F. Meany, Jr. entitled "Merchant and Redcoat: The Papers of John Gordon Macomb, July 1757 to June 1760" (Ph.D. diss., Fordham University, 1989). The career of carpenter Alexander Forsyth (5904) provides a representative example of the adaptability of Scottish émigrés.

14. The acculturation of the descendants of Irish garrison soldiers is documented by their participation in the activities of St. Peter's Anglican Church or in their moving to the Dutch church when they married the daughters of New Netherland families. Properly reconstructed, the Irish nevertheless achieved neither wealth nor prominence in pre-Revolutionary Albany. Thomas Barry (1821), once a baker, profitted from wartime trade, and stood at the head of a commercially oriented group of recently arrived Irish and French Catholics who came together in the Catholic church. See John J. Dillon, *The Historic Story of St. Mary's, Albany, N.Y.* (New York, 1933). Irish immigration to and settlement in Albany was a constant trickle from the end of the war to the 1840s when it escalated greatly. More than a hundred Catholic Irish families were established in the city prior to the "Potato Famine" migration.

The French were represented by a smaller group. The Pruyn family, the De Garmos, and the Bassets were Calvinists and had been resident in Albany for several generations. Few new settlers of French ancestry entered the community until the 1770s when a number of conspicuous "French Merchants" purchased the right to do business in the city. This profile is derived from an assessment roll for 1779 in the "Gerrit Yates Lansing Papers" at the New York State Library and from a list of "Freedoms Purchased, 1781," in the Albany "City Records." Copies of both documents are filed at the CAP office. This group was Catholic, and included the merchant John Maley (1058), an Alsatian and the most prominent of Albany's French-speaking enclave. Fewer than a dozen French Catholic families migrated up the Hudson and were established in the community before 1800. Albany did not receive an influx of French Canadians comparable to that of other northern cities.

15. Without a full-time pastor, colonial Albany's Lutheran parish was composed of farmer members who often availed themselves of services at St. Peters. After 1700, few prominent city residents belonged to the Lutheran Church since support of the Dutch Reformed church was a common denominator of almost all of Albany's best families regardless of heritage. The Germans who settled in the community after 1750, however, were very inclined toward Lutheran membership. Their participation is documented by the records of the First Lutheran Church, printed as *The Manual of the First Lutheran Church in the City of Albany* (Albany, 1871). For exemplification of the German experience in Albany in the era of the Constitution, see the cases of Paul Hoghstrasser (8494) and his son Paul (8495), Conrad Ruby (1056), and Andries Abel (1768). Each of these first generation city residents became patriarchs of large families that became closely connected through marriage. Albany's German-speaking enclave was larger than the French but more difficult to comprehend because the German inclination toward agriculture drew them away from the city.

16. Stefan Bielinski, "The Jacksons, the Lattimores, and the Schuylers: Three Albany Families and the emergence of an African-American Middle Class in Post Revolutionary Society," a working paper presented at history conferences during 1989, and the sources cited therin. See also, Shane White, "Pinkster in Albany, 1803: A Contemporary Description," *New York History* 70 (April 1989), 191–99. Instructive in the area of slave/owner relations in urban areas is Thomas J. Davis, *A Rumor of Revolt: The "Great Negro Plot" in Colonial New York* (New York, 1985), esp. chaps. 1–3. Dr. Samuel Stringer offered what has become the classic explanation of the reasons that slavery no longer worked in the north in a letter to Jellis Fonda, dated March 2, 1770, "Albany Papers—Stringer," New York Public Library.

17. The topic of inheritance and related issues are most ably discussed by David E. Narrett. See his "Patterns of Inheritance in Colonial New York City, 1664–1775: A Study in the History of the Family" (Ph.D. diss. Cornell University, 1981), and particularly "Preparation for Death and Provision for the Living: Notes on New York Wills (1665–1760)," *New York History* 57 (October 1976), 417–37. The latter source first called our attention to the potential of probate records for New York community studies. The Colonial Albany Project expects to find estate disposition records for each city householder. To date we have identified over 500 wills, inventories, and letters of administration. These have been assembled from a number of sources and repositories described in the "Probate Records" section of the CAP "Guide." Copies of each are filed at the CAP office. Most often, testators evaded primogeniture requirements by making a nominal birthright bequest, divided the estate either equally or on the basis of need, and permitted the widow use of all or part of the estate during her widowhood.

For independent women, see CAP biographies of Catherine Douw (2067), Rachel Douw (2168), Ann Beekman (3895) and Genevieve Maase Lydius (1473), who lived during this period as the head of the landmark house on the corner of State and North Pearl Streets in the absence of her husband.

18. An appreciation of the volume and diversity of activities that made up the "boom town" atmosphere that characterized Albany during the latter part of the eighteenth century can be derived from the variety of advertisements appearing in local newspapers, from travellers accounts, and from the minutes of the city council. See also, "The Trade of Albany, 1784–1796," in Arthur J. Weise, *The History of the City of Albany, New York* (Albany, 1884), 386–423.

19. A profile of the rise of the state government established in Albany can be pieced together from a survey of the records of its agencies held at the New York State Archives. Among these are Land Papers, papers of the secretary of state, the board of regents, council of appointment, and, of fundamental importance, the papers of Governor George Clinton. Edward Countryman's, "Legislative Government in Revolutionary New York, 1777–1788" (Ph.D. diss. Cornell University, 1971), provides a framework for understanding the workings of state government. Particularly helpful for the rise of higher education in the state and of the Regents during this period is Bruce B. Detlefsen, *A Popular History of the Origins of the Regents of the University of the State of New York* (Albany, 1975).

The son of a one-time privateer, Stephen Lush (1753–1825) held an M.A. from King's College, was a protegé of William Smith, Jr., and had been imprisoned on one of the "Jersey prison ships." The life of this fascinating character is chronicled in CAP case 416. See 1047, for the complementary career of Richard Lush.

20. The "Graphics Archive" at the CAP includes copies of all extant depictions of early Albany buildings and streetscapes. Of particular interest in articulating the street plan and documenting the built environment during this period are the maps made of the community by Simeon De Witt (1794) which was produced in several significantly varied forms; by John Bogert (1792); and those sketched by the schoolteacher Simeon Baldwin in 1782. Copies of more specialized street maps from the period 1780–1810 originally in the city engineer's office also have been scrutinized. See *World Our Fathers Made: A Survey of the Records of Local Governments in the County of Albany, New York During the Constitutional Era, 1783–1815,* compiled by Tracy B. Grimm (Albany, 1988), 17–19. The CAP is collecting copies of different versions of the James Eights drawings of Albany and continues to discover new materials. Copies of all documentary resources are on file at the CAP office.

21. The unimproved condition of the Albany riverfront is depicted visually in the "Burgiss" view of 1717 and portrayed graphically in the Roemer map of 1698; the British army maps of Albany during the 1750s in the "Crown Collection" at the New York State Library; in the "Brasier Map" of 1765, which shows the first offshore dockage that would emerge several decades later as the "Albany Basin"; the Robert Yates map of 1770; and the Simeon De Witt map of 1794. A copy or published print of each of these resources is filed at the CAP office. The city corporation's efforts on behalf of construction of the docks and other waterfront developments are chronicled in the "City Records," common council minutes held at the Albany County Hall of Records, microfilm copy filed at the CAP office.

This social geography is informed by the above named sources; by a number of cartographic resources including the so-called "Sprague Plan" of 1764, which designated uptown streets in honor of the royal family and British notables; Simeon Baldwin's sketch made in 1782; the Bogart street maps of the 1790s; and the so-called "Mellius Collection" of maps originally held by the city engineer's office; by descriptive information recovered from Albany newspapers of the period; probate and real estate records; and city assessment rolls. Copies of all relevant documents are held at the CAP office.

22. A roster of Albany vessels and Albany sailors engaged in the Hudson River trade is being compiled from sources beginning with *An Account of Her Majesty's Revenue in the Province of New York, 1701–09: The Customs Record of Early Colonial New York*, ed. by Leo Hershkowitz, et al. (Ridgewood, N.J., 1966), and ultimately will comprehend official documents, business papers, newspaper advertisements and notices, military pension applications, the Albany city directories which began in 1813, records of local government including rosters of jurymen and voters, which provide occupational information. At this point, some information has been collected from each of these sources to support this general profile. The narrative pension application of Captain John Bogart (1761–1853) (case 6121) submitted by him in 1833 represents an outstanding example of the potential of these resources. A copy of the affidavit from the National Archives is filed at the CAP office.

The broad community implications of this trade can be appreciated from the "Account of Sales of the Cargo of the Sloop *Olive Branch*" captained by Abraham Bloodgood (case 7351) to Antigua in 1770. The ship's manifest identified more than thirty different Albany people as consignees of more than a hundred commodities, ranging from flour to staves to horses, fish, fowl, and other food items. The return trip from Antigua and St. Christophers brought rum, limes, cotton, and cash. The list is printed in *Annals of Albany*, 1:258–61.

Abraham Eights (case 7800) was Albany's foremost sailmaker. His home on Dock Street next to the home of Captain Stewart Dean (5135) marked the center of a growing shiplifting section during the postwar years.

23. While carters were licensed to haul cargoes within the city from its early days, the extant records do not approach those that inform Graham R. Hodges, *The New York City Cartmen, 1667–1850* (New York, 1986). Instead, more casual references to carters and wagonners, who carried freight and produce to and from Albany, are scattered through "The City Records," accounts and survey documents, and literary sources. The volume of overland carriage appeared to increase during the wartime 1750s as the widespread nature of wagon ownership was revealed by the British as they pressed Albany haulers into service. Several families, however, seem to have developed a freighting tradition. These include the Vandenberghs, Radcliffs, Bradts, and the Archers.

24. Albany's pre-industrial production economy is profiled in Stefan Bielinski, "A Middling Sort: Artisans and Tradesman in Colonial Albany," forthcoming from New-York Historical Society. The colonial roots of the juncture of production and commerce stem from the ability of prominent merchants to secure supply contracts from the province and then agreeing with a number of local artisans to produce a quantity of boots, belts, or blankets. See Bielinski, "How a City Worked: Occupations in Colonial Albany," *Selected Rensselaerswyck Papers* (forthcoming from the New Netherland Project, 1990).

25. For one-time blacksmith Gerrit Witbeck, one of the new tradesmen able to become a proprietor, see case 1791. The second nail factory was underwritten by John Stevenson, John De Peyster Douw, and Henry Ten Eyck.

26. For James Caldwell (1747–1829), see 7509. Caldwell and his family were the first settlers of Caldwell, later Lake George, in Warren County. Caldwell's major factory complex was located north of the city, upstream from the Van Rennsselaer manor house. A contemporary print detailing that operation is in the collection of the New York State Museum. Other descriptive materials on Caldwell's extensive manufacturing enterprises have been compiled and are filed with James Caldwell's case history (7509). For Mc Clallen and Maley, see cases 725 and 1058, respectively. Batterman of Boston was not a city resident. Instead, he resided near the glassworks he operated in Guilderland, about ten miles west of the river.

27. The inferior and declining standard of living of artisans and other producers is revealed in a number of extant city assessment rolls which fix their real estate holdings in the bottom half and their personal property in the bottom quartile of the community. Never among the community's leading citizens but conspicuous participants in community activities, by the 1790s, those in traditional crafts and trades typically lived in less affluent corners of the city, often found their sons employed in more service-oriented occupations, and played diminished and still declining roles in the activities of city government and in other participant groups.

28. The mayoral careers of Abraham Yates, Jr. (1724–96), and General Abraham Ten Broeck (1734–1810) are detailed in CAP biographies 2 and 6, respectively. After the mid-1780s, the minutes of the Albany Common Council reveal an expanding scope of concern and escalating volume of activity. Systematic record-keeping, however, seems to have dated from the late 1790s with the first extant comprehensive lists of licenses, fire companies, "permanent poor," and other documents including maps, deeds, and assessment rolls. See "The City Records," manuscript held at the Albany County Hall of Records; microfilm copy at CAP office.

29. The most demonstrative roster of Albany boosters were the 99 notables who subscribed sums up to 500 pounds for the establishment of a college in Albany in 1794. The list includes all but a few of the city's most civic-minded; printed in *Annals of Albany*, 8:131–32. See also the signers of a legislative petition for library incorporation dated January 21, 1797, in the "Miscellaneous Manuscripts" at the New-York Historical Society. Copies of the rosters of directors and investors in the first Albany banks and other cooperative ventures are filed in the CAP resources database.

Oliver Phelps. Painted, 1822, by T. L. Dallathies. Courtesy of the On-tario County Historical Society, Canandaigua, New York.

Wilderness Investment: The New York Frontier During the Federal Period

William H. Siles

During the federal era, civilization expanded well beyond New York's line of Colonial settlements. The so-called Fort Stanwix line, artificially imposed by British ministers in 1768, stretched southward across New York, from Rome to the Pennsylvania border near Binghamton, and was intended by America's rulers to legally separate Indian lands from American settlements. But American victory in the Revolutionary War transferred power from the British to state and federal officials which resulted in an American re-evaluation of the old Stanwix line. At the same time, Indian lands west of Rome were much talked about by soldiers who fought in central and western New York under General Sullivan in 1779. After the Revolutionary War, stories of rich lands, flourishing orchards, plentiful water and abundant woods and wildlife circulated in eastern cities as far south as Baltimore. But the center of interest was in New England, New York, and Philadelphia where businessmen, some of whom had been colonial leaders, took note of approximately ten million acres stretching between Rome and Lake Erie and awaited the disposition of the Indian land claims there and the establishment of political control over it by New York State.

When the Confederation government established its authority over the state's Indian lands in 1784, the State of New York advanced its claim of political jurisdiction in a treaty signed by Governor George Clinton and representatives of the Six Nations at Fort Stanwix in 1784. Then, four million acres were actually signed over to the state by the Cayuga Nation in a treaty at Fort

Stanwix in 1789. This treaty was quickly renounced by the Indians and remained in dispute during the 1790s.[1] At the same time, Massachusetts, Pennsylvania, and Connecticut demanded a part of the western land on the basis of their colonial charters that specified jurisdiction from "sea to sea." New York State representatives successfully defended their right against every claim but Massachusetts. Representatives of the two states met at Hartford, Connecticut, in late 1786, and agreed to compromise. New York retained political sovereignty over the disputed territory while Massachusetts got the right to buy it from the Indians and to sell it to settlers. In a series of clever agreements, the Yankees also got New York to agree not to levy a tax on the land for fifteen years from the time Massachusetts conferred the title to the purchase. And the Massachusetts legislature got the right to dispose of the "right to buy" preemption as it saw fit. These concessions made the lands especially attractive to businessmen, while Massachusetts, left nearly bankrupt by the Revolutionary War, viewed a sale of its right as a way to generate badly needed revenue.[2]

Investors were waiting for a chance to control land west of the old Stanwix line. During the late 1780s, there was very little opportunity to invest money in ventures with growth potential or the promise of steady and substantial return on investment. Trade with Europe, especially trade with Great Britain, proved very risky. Between 1783 and 1786, American traders sent out huge orders for British and Western European goods, but the profits realized by Americans were nil. Abnormal demand in England limited supplies, and credit purchases forced up prices.[3] Large transfers of specie to England to pay the bills, commonly in gold and silver coinage, drained America of a necessary supply of circulating medium. The result was "anarchy of commerce," as James Madison termed it in March, 1786, "a continuance of the unfavorable balance on it, which by draining us of our metals, furnishes pretexts for pernicious substitution of paper money. . . . In fact most of our political evils may be traced to our commercial ones."[4] This is why the twin threat of inflation and a commercial depression drove many men of the propertied, creditor class away from trade and into investing in banking stock and in lands.

Of the two, bank stock appeared more attractive. The low prices of American goods in European and American markets, shortages of hard money, private debts, and relatively high taxes made the American economy fragile. Although the states did not have enough cash to stimulate business, the three private banks then in existence were equipped with sufficient funds to make loans to selected individuals, which guaranteed a stable and highly profitable return on investment. The banks, including the Bank of North America, the Massachusetts Bank, and the Bank of New York, all in existence in 1784, prospered during the 1780s. Each paid dividends ranging from 2.5 to 14 percent, and each bank succeeded in maintaining specie payments on all its notes and deposits. However, loans were confined to a select number of local merchants with whom the officers were acquainted.[5] In this way, bankers and investors protected themselves from accumulating bad debts and maintained a flow of specie within a tight circle of business acquaintances.

Another attraction for investors was wild land, especially lands available in Ohio and western New York. "Do you think to prevent the emigration from a barren country loaded with taxes and impoverished with debts, to the most luxurious soil in the world?" an Ohio pioneer asked an eastern friend in 1787.[6] This was impossible to do, judged one potential land investor who calculated that a profitable market probably existed in the re-sale of frontier land, its commercial development, or both. The opportunity to settle on good, tax-free land would attract at least "2 or 3,000 settlers" from barren New England during the first year alone, noted Oliver Phelps in 1788.[7] The backland of New York could attract people from every state, he said, "but especially from New England, where they have a great spirit of emigration."[8] William Temple Franklin, commenting in 1790 on the prospects for investment in wild lands, observed that population along the Atlantic coast would double every twenty years, and "quite apart from European immigration, speculators could depend upon a great movement every year from the seaboard back into the interior." Franklin estimated that each year of the 1790s would see 50,000 young people looking for homes.[9]

Such predictions were among the factors that aroused the interest of speculators in western lands. Phelps, a veteran land speculator from Massachusetts, who had derived his wealth from merchandizing and the wholesaling of agricultural commodities in New York City before the Revolution, believed that between $50,000 and $250,000 profit could be made after one year if proper measures were taken to foster settlement on a speculative frontier land purchase.[10] In light of American business activity in the late eighteenth century, potential profits such as these might appear fabulous and very enticing to men caught in an unstable economic and political environment. With very few options available to them at this time, men of business and property watched carefully as the Indian lands in upstate New York passed into the hands of the State of New York. Oliver Phelps, in 1787, a staunch believer in land speculation and a resident of Massachusetts, waited until the Commonwealth obtained the right to purchase Indian land in central and western New York and then put into action a plan to create an investor's market in frontier land and to realize profit from land sales to settlers.[11]

Shortly after representatives of Massachusetts announced their acquisition of the preemption right, groups of investors acting as individuals and in coalition made inquiry concerning the price and quantity of lands available for purchase. Oliver Phelps surveyed the field of bidders and concluded that a coalition of New Englanders, carefully selected, would carry the bid. Late in 1787, Phelps submitted a request to the Massachusetts General Court to purchase one million acres at five cents an acre.[12] This met such opposition in the Senate, with "so many person's eyes and ears wide open, propagating great stories about the value of these lands" that Phelps requested that his request be postponed until early 1788.[13] During these same winter months of 1787–88, a competing company of investors in New York State complicated matters by attempting to gain control of Indian lands on their own. Forming a group called the New York Company of Associates, and acting without the authority of the New York legislature, these men persuaded leaders of the Seneca Nation to sign a long lease which gave the company control over two million acres of land between the Seneca Lake and Genesee River. A second lease, signed by the sachems of the Onondaga and the Oneida, ceded control of Indian land between Oneida Lake and Fort Stanwix. By January 8, 1788, when the second lease was signed, an actual market in upstate wild lands had been created by the New York Associates. Although the leases were quickly condemned by Governor George Clinton and repudiated by the legislature,

Phelps and his associate formed a coalition with the New York Company to guarantee a clear title to all the land they purchased.[14] Phelps and his principal associates also agreed to bid on six million rather than one million acres of land. When the bids were opened in March 1788, the House of Representatives approved a sale to Phelps and his associates of six million acres at a price of $300,000 in Massachusetts currency. This price amounted to two cents an acre, or a cost below that of the original bid in 1787.[15]

The Phelps Associates were well pleased with the outcome of the negotiation. The original thirteen stock holders—including Nathaniel Gorham of Charleston, Massachusetts; Jeremiah Wadsworth of Hartford, Connecticut; Thomas Russell, a great merchant of Charleston; John Brown of Providence, Rhode Island; and numerous other locally prominent judges, merchants, and doctors—held two-thirds of the 120 shares of company stock. One-third of the shares belonged to men such as John Livingston of Hudson, New York, who were prominent members of the New York Company of Associates.[16] Phelps planned carefully when he allocated shares in his land company. He reserved seventy-two shares for himself and Nathaniel Gorham, giving each man thirty-six shares and equal footing in the enterprise. He did this partly to encourage Gorham to drop his plan to bid on his own and partly to attach Gorham closely to the project. Nathaniel Gorham's standing in Massachusetts politics was very high during the late 1780s. He was a judge of the Middlesex County court of Common Pleas, was appointed a member of the Governor's Council, was Superintendent of Revenue of Massachusetts, and was a commonwealth representative to the Constitutional Convention in 1787.[17] Gorham's political influence was substantial at the time Phelps made his bid on the New York lands and he received extra shares for his contributions.

In addition to the original thirteen shareholders who owned stock prior to Phelps's purchase of the redemption right in 1788, twenty-two additional investors purchased the remaining forty shares by the end of 1789. A share sold for £500 New York currency or $1,250 in 1788 and rose steadily until it reached a value of £753 New York, or $1,882, in 1791. Each share was equal to 50,000 acres. On this basis, the Phelps-Gorham Land Company, as it was called, was capitalized at $150,000 New York

Nathaniel Gorham. Painter and date unconfirmed. Courtesy of the County of Ontario, Canandaigua, New York.

currency in 1789. This amount of cash and the broad spectrum of stockholders is an indication that investors in the northeast anticipated quick profits from a land speculation and land development scheme in the west when they could not find suitable opportunities in more common investments such as trade. Oliver Phelps's grand design of combining both speculation and development in the purchase and resale of New York's wilderness apparently was deemed sensible and practical to these men of property. If a measure of confidence in a venture can be determined by the amount an individual is willing to invest, $1,250 a share was a signal of esteem. It was the equivalent of the net worth of an average farmer in Massachusetts in 1790.[18]

Phelps completed an initial purchase of 2.5 million acres from the Seneca Nation in July 1788. The land company was then in business, and the investment strategy of its principal director ready to be put to the test.[19] At the time of the Indian purchase, Phelps demanded the entire six million acres, but discovered that the leaders of the six nations were stubborn in their view that all the land west of the Genesee, except for a half-million acre "mill lot" at present-day Rochester, New York, was not for sale. Deeply disappointed, Phelps bought all he was able and determined to return when prospects were brighter. In the interim, he put into action his plans for squeezing big profits from nearly valueless properties.

Phelps's investment strategy proceeded in two phases, the first of which was the actual purchase and parcelling out to investors of all the lands he acquired from the Indians. Distribution of land was done on the bases of surveys which he directed during the summer and autumn of 1788. Phelps's land purchase was found, upon inspection, to be a generally rectangular configuration, forty-three miles wide and eighty-three miles long, thus capable of accommodating townships six miles square. The Company could sell land by the township and the profits collected divided among the stock holders. Then, in order to attract buyers and to tap the huge potential market for western lands in the east, Phelps proposed his second phase, the survey and promotion of desirable villages and towns amongst the townships, to drive up land values and to help sell off less desirable properties.[20]

The creation of these "city-towns," as he referred to them, was necessary to stimulate actual settlement. A "city-town" was a village site located within a choice township. He identified several such locations on his purchase as sites for these settlements. One site was located at the head of Seneca Lake, another at the head of Canandaigua Lake, and a third on the east bank of the Genesee River. The village-town configuration fostered a concentration of people, increased the quantity of trade in the locale, and encouraged the development of businesses everywhere.[21] Phelps chose the land at the head of Canandaigua Lake as his principal village-town township, designated it the county seat of his newly formed county of Ontario in 1789, and planned its development. This village site was in the center of his lands, situated on a main east-west Indian trail and connected by a series of water routes to the Mohawk River. It therefore qualified in all respects as the principal focus of the second phase of Phelps's investment strategy. Canandaigua, an Indian word meaning "The Chosen Place," was chosen again by Phelps to be the organizing point around which New York's frontier land would develop. Planted early and well in advance of settlement, Canandaigua was an example of what historian Richard C. Wade has noted as a spearhead of the frontier, thrust forward, anchored, and awaiting a pioneering population.[22]

Throughout 1788 and 1789, Phelps optimistically promoted the creation of the village and town of Canandaigua. His company cut pathways through the wilderness so farmers could reach the "Promised Lands" as easily as possible. Water navigation was improved by the clearing out of debris, and wide bridges were constructed over swampy lands to facilitate migration.[23] Surveyors were then sent to the "Chosen Place" to map out the town and village, oversee the clearing of the outlet on Canandaigua Lake and to erect a land office.[24] The company surveyors, William Walker and Israel Chapin, identified a pleasant sloping hill on the west bank of the outlet with a picturesque view of Canandaigua Lake and agreed that it was the best spot to site the main portion of the new village. In two months' time, from mid-September to mid-November 1788, the men surveyed 120-acre lots in a straight northeast direction from the lake and divided the land behind into 120 twenty-acre lots. The survey was arranged in such a way as to preserve for future settlers an unobstructed view of the lake. In the center of the village, Walker surveyed a wide six-rod road that led to a large public square. It was believed that the wide, straight road connecting the lake and the village green would impress visitors and lead to rapid settlement.[25] When Walker and his party departed Canandaigua in November, the outline of what Phelps believed to be a profitable venture was in place. A former Indian site was ready to become home to a new civilization of American property owners, farmers, and businessmen.

Although much more surveying, road building, and building construction was required to make the village and the region flourish, the Phelps-Gorham Purchase was opened for sales and settlement in the spring of 1789. Townships sold for an average of 20 cents an acre or $4,000 for an entire town. In Canandaigua, village lots, which Phelps rearranged into ten-acre front lots and thirty-acre back lots were priced at $1.00 an acre. Farm lots, which averaged 100 acres apiece, were priced at 50 cents an acre. Equivalent lands in New England sold for $10.00 to $20.00 an acre and good lands in eastern New York sold for $8.00 to $10.00 an acre. Phelps therefore believed that his prices were an "inducement" to development. In addition, Phelps instructed his land agents to accept unsecured notes as a down payment and to offer purchasers three year's time to pay off the balance on the property.[26] Finally, agents were told to grant mortgage deeds instead of tenant contracts when a down payment was made. A mortgage deed enabled purchasers to claim equity in the property if it was sold before it was paid off, and mortgage deeds, in contrast to tenant contracts, carried legal rights which made it difficult for a mortgage holder to evict a property owner or to deny him a clear title to the land.[27]

These policies were supplemented by others which were aimed at building a handsome as well as a populous frontier village. Village residents were required to erect decent dwelling houses on their main street lots as soon as practical. Phelps built a fine house for himself on a corner lot near the square as an example of his idea of "decency." During the spring of 1789, twelve original investors purchased property in the village and established residences. Their purpose was to pursue private business activity and to sell company land, but their presence boosted Canandaigua's value among potential settlers and land speculators. As a result, land sold well. In the village forty-two lots sold during the first year of operation, and in the town twenty-one farm lots were deeded by the company. Five farm families actually moved onto their lands, and eleven families took up residence in the village. After one year of sales, the change taking place in the wilderness was striking. John H. Jones, a settler who later became a frontier judge, wrote "When we left Canandaigua in the fall of '88, there was not a solitary person there; when I returned fourteen months afterwards the place was full of people—residents, surveyors, explorers, adventurers, houses were going up; it was a busy, thriving place."[28] The Phelps strategy of creating a market for lands among investors and settlers appeared to be effective. Lands were selling and land values were holding firm or actually rising.

In 1788, Phelps predicted that investors could depend upon the company selling every good township in the Genesee Country by the end of 1789, and the results proved him correct. By the end of 1789, the company actually sold forty-six out of fifty available townships at an average price of 16 cents an acre for a total of $125,000, inclusive of Canandaigua sales.[29] Expenses were calculated by Phelps at half this amount. However, all of the sales were made on credit, which reflected the country's dire shortage of currency, so that little money was actually received. The company was thus a financial success on paper, but its coffers held only a small amount of the money needed to meet the first of three installments due the Commonwealth of Massachusetts at the end of 1789. The commonwealth intended that Phelps and his shareholders pay off its debt in inflated Massachusetts currency. By doing so, the company would help retire this debt and at the same time place into circulation notes and specie with higher value. But this plan was thwarted when Alexander Hamilton, the new Secretary of the Treasury in the Washington administration, favored a plan to have the federal government reclaim state notes at par value. The anticipation of such a plan in 1789 among holders of near worthless state currency, caused the value of the currency to rise just as the company's first note was due.[30] When Hamilton's plan was announced in 1790, state securities were near face value, and the supply had dried up. Phelps had calculated the cost of acquiring Massachusetts note at 37 cents on bills worth $2.50 face value. But in late 1789, these prices stood at $1.25. Phelps needed about $100,000 to make his installment, but had collected only about $42,000 from the land sales. When Phelps failed to make his payment, he and nine of his shareholders, who were residents of Massachusetts were sued by the state in January 1790.[31] During the ensuing weeks, the company members and Massachusetts reached an agreement. The company agreed to allow the state to become a partner in the business, share in the profits, and oversee the company's finances in return for the state's forgiveness of two-thirds of the three installments. The company would continue to develop the land they owned as long as they paid off the first installment on the contract. Massachusetts would then re-assume ownership of the preemption right to all the land west of the Genesee River and resell it as it wished. The agreement was approved in March 1790, and the company continued in business.[32] During March, Robert Morris, the Philadelphia financier who had directed America's fiscal matters during the Revolution, offered to buy all the unsold lands on the company's books east of the Genesee and acquired a substantial portion of the pre-emption right to all the lands on the west side of the river. This sale was made in August 1790, and added such a substantial amount to the company's income that it allowed all the shareholders to realize a dividend on their stock.[33] When the Phelps and Gorham Company settled accounts with Massachusetts and then disbanded in 1791, the members walked away with money in their pockets, but just as importantly, they left behind a sturdy foundation, which enabled Canandaigua and communities like it to flourish.[34]

Because of his huge land holdings in Canandaigua and elsewhere in the Phelps-Gorham Purchases, Oliver Phelps remained involved in the region's development until his death in Canandaigua in 1809. However, he continued to press his business view that land investment and community development in upstate New York was the very best way propertied individuals could make money. "The best land [is] still under the Indians" near Buffalo, he wrote, and "if the lands while new and encumbered with Indians will sell at 1/4 [16 cents], what will the lands that are much better in natural situation sell for. . .?[35] The lands west of the Genesee "will fetch double the sum of 1/4 [16 cents] now got for Genesee lands in 5 years."[36] Phelps, the land broker and consummate investor, set his sights on future profits ever westward.

What was it like living in a newly created frontier community located hundreds of miles from home? Canandaigua, the community in which Phelps chose to reside in 1802, represented all of the attributes, both positive and negative, encountered by settlers during the pioneering process in upstate New York. When settlers crossed the old Fort Stanwix line at Rome, New York, they entered a land of scarcity, disease, and danger. But the land was cheap, fertile, and beautifully located near abundant supplies of water from lakes and rivers and filled with every kind of natural resource a settler could use. Opportunity to own good land and to create a new society enticed pioneers to try their luck. But the hard work, sickness, isolation, and danger associated with settlement planted in the midst of Indian territory far from home sent many packing. Those who remained did prosper and eventually owned large farms and attractive homes to pass on to their children. Those who struggled to create a community in New York's western wilderness were amply repaid in material and social benefits.

The initial establishment of a community involved a settler in a fierce struggle with nature and demanded energy, self-discipline, and uncommon courage. The mere location of Canandaigua, in the center of the Phelps-Gorham Purchase, 150 miles from Albany, its nearest market, made settlement extremely difficult. Pathways leading into the wilderness were inadequate for year-round travel, and except for winter, most trade traveled slowly over water routes. The cost of operating small batteaus that carried a limited volume of cargo, and the time needed to transport goods in and out of the wilderness were factors in creating scarcity on the frontier for many years. Thus, bartering among neighbors and between settlers and suppliers quickly developed and remained in effect throughout the 1790s. Families exchanged labor, furs, and agricultural commodities for the necessities of life, oftentimes getting credit when the value of the barter would not cover the bill. Articles available for purchase were only the basic necessities needed to survive. Flour, sugar, salt, tea, plates, cloth, coffee, beef, butter, and eggs were sold in merchants' shops. Children looked forward to having an occasional piece of chocolate when it became available, and young women bought ribbon to dress up a hat. But there were no other special treats imported during the early years. Books, newspapers, Bibles, and even pens, paper, and ink were in very short supply. Basic services such as mail delivery and stage travel, taken for granted by eastern families, would not become available until reliable communication was established with eastern cities.[37]

Two technical achievements, the construction of a primitive canal on the Mohawk River and the completion of a turnpike road, helped ease Canandaigua's problems and contributed to community growth. In 1790, a trip from Canandaigua to Albany took twenty-one days by water. Small batteaux poled by several men had to make three portages around waterfalls and the crew had to carry their craft one mile between the end of Wood Creek at Rome and the Mohawk River. A company called the Western Inland Lock Company built three locks which joined the creek to the river in 1796. As a consequence, sixteen-ton boats could pass through with little delay, and the cost of transport westward dropped from between $75 and $100 a ton to $35 in 1796 when the canal opened.[38]

Phelps and his fellow investors with homes in Canandaigua also fought for the construction of a wide, level, all-weather road between the Purchase and the Mohawk. When the state refused to build one, Phelps associated with other investors and land agents and chartered a private company to build a turnpike road from Utica to Canandaigua. This project was begun in 1800 and completed in 1804 when it opened for business. The Seneca Turnpike, as it was called, enabled tonnage rates to drop to $1.83 per ton and reduced travel time from Canandaigua to Utica and Rome from ten days to five.

Many advantages accrued to Canandaiguans as a result of these developments. Swifter and cheaper transportation permitted regular mail service between eastern cities and frontier communities. Until 1802, when Postmaster-General Gideon Granger revamped the mail, mail service was nearly nonexistent. Twice a month post riders from Albany and Canandaigua met in Utica and exchanged mail. Granger contracted with private carriers to run stages to Canandaigua twice a week and a post office was designated in the village to handle the volume of mail generated by its growing population. When the mails were made regular, newspaper subscriptions increased. A delivery list for 1810 contained twenty-six papers originating in small Massachusetts towns like Worcester, Stockbridge, Pittsfield, and Greenfield, and large cities like Boston, Baltimore, New York, and Philadelphia.[39] Canandaiguans were fortunate in that Gideon Granger was a personal friend of Oliver Phelps and that he chose to become a resident in the village in 1814. This personal contact no doubt helped the community to get reliable service at an early date.

Transportation improvements also affected the quantity and quality of goods and services available in the frontier community. The number of businesses and the variety of available goods increased at a startling rate between the first years of settlement and the early 1800s. In 1789, Walker's log cabin was the only structure in the village. By 1805, the village alone contained forty-five business establishments. In 1791, a settler was hard pressed to purchase a pepper or a pound of coffee. But after 1800, a variety of luxury goods were available, including silk gloves, silk shawls, fancy silk hose, wine glasses, and many other fancy items. In 1802, a traveler from Suffield, Connecticut, reported that Canandaigua's main store contained ''a large store of goods, equal to all the stores in Suffield . . . 10, 15 & 20 people are constantly in the store. The store kept open till 9 & 10 o'clock at night.'' And because this store served a wide region, it was common for the proprietors to sell about a thousand dollars worth of goods a day.[40]

The successful development of merchandising was but one manifestation of economic change in Canandaigua during the first decade of settlement. As late as 1796, the village had only a few taverns and inns, a couple of small stores, a distillery, several smiths, and a leather goods manufacturer. By 1804, Canandaigua boasted a number of watchmakers and jewelers, tailors, and shoemakers, bakers, and hairdressers, and a well-stocked book and stationery store. In 1806, a drugstore opened for business, and two newspapers were published in the village.[41] Farm women were attracted to displays of straw bonnets, turtle shell combs, and leather shoes. Almost overnight the memory of shopping at a log hut filled only with cheap calicoes began to fade. The availability of plates, vest buttons, and fancy handkerchiefs were marks of the rapid development of their town and village. Life was always getting better. But there were some things that Canandaiguans did not want changed. One of these—a source of pride among Canandaiguans—was the physical beauty of the village.

Phelps's plan for Canandaigua's development included the idea of building a community that was visually attractive. A well laid out main street that offered a view of Canandaigua Lake, lined with attractive and well built residences and businesses, served as a promotion for the community. Phelps believed that good buildings represented a sound investment since land values rose as new people were attracted to the village. He according-ly required villagers to erect a decent dwelling house within one year of their settlement or stand to forfeit the land. Lots overrun with bushes and trees were ordered removed by the owner "so as to afford a good and clear prospect of said lake from the public square." Phelp's policy was enforceable because he wrote his terms into the mortgage deeds issued to land pur-chasers. As a result, frames for houses, farms, and stores quickly dwarfed small log cabins, and although shortage of building materials slowed construction, by 1800 many substantial and attractive buildings were in place. These structures lent grace and dignity to the small community and conveyed to visitors a sense of growth and prosperity.[42]

The wide sloping main street extended from the lake past handsome structures to the public square in the center of the village. At this point, visitors gazed upon another of Phelps's projects—public buildings to serve the needs of the residents of Ontario County, which he helped create in 1789. The Ontario County court building, built in 1794, was a fine two-story frame building with an attractive spire on top. Phelps demanded that the building complement the village, and to retain control he lent the village $200 in lieu of taxes and also contributed glass, paint, nails, and sawmill service as well. When completed the courthouse was a significant achievement among Phelps's many accomplishments.[43]

A wilderness life did not appeal to most people, a fact reflected in the effort to introduce conveniences into communi-ties like Canandaigua. Descriptions of pioneering in 1789 state that nearly every person living in the woods was either con-nected with the Phelps-Gorham enterprise or peddling and trading cheap trinkets. In that year, for example, the tiny population was composed mostly of transient land speculators, Indian traders, Indians, peddlers, and surveyors mixed with a handful of actual settlers. Such a mixture made for a cosmopolitan population in the county, which had 1,049 resi-dents in 1790, and in Canandaigua.[44] The settlers were of diverse geographic, social, and economic backgrounds. Wealthy investors, such as Phelps, mingled with Indian traders, farmers, and blacksmiths. Several of the early pioneers were college-educated and one was a doctor. There were Congregationalists, Episcopalians, non-believers, and Baptists among the group, and diversity allowed strangers to find a place for themselves in the new society in the wilderness.

Diversity also marked the demographic composition of the pioneer settlements. A pattern was established in the early years when families rather than single people chose to make permanent residence on the frontier. Married men with families were most numerous in the village and in the town. Though family size ranged from one to eight members, the average size was six. And age was not a factor in selecting people for life in the woods. Youthful men, but not raw youths, tended to pick up and move west. The average age for all villagers at the time of arrival was thirty-two. But the range of age was very broad. Older men and young worked side by side with those in the prime of life. Men aged sixty-one shared hardships with those of thirty-one and twenty-one, and these variations reflected how receptive, how untrammelled, frontier life was at the beginning. Just about everyone with health and ambition could try his hand. No one needed to feel excluded from the chance to own property and perhaps to grow wealthy.[45]

Such ventures were not, however, without difficulties. Even Canandaigua, the rising star among frontier settlements in upstate New York, was beset by problems related to such matters as Indian relations and frontier disease, which took the edge off pioneering enthusiasm and even threatened to turn the little frontier community into a ghost town. The Indian population in upstate New York in 1792 was estimated by federal agents at 3,823. These Indians were members of the Six Nations of Indians and lived between the Mohawk River and Fort Niagara. Of these, 1,800 were Seneca Tribesmen who lived within fifty miles of Canandaigua. Uneasiness among some Indian leaders over Phelps's treaty in 1788 and resistance to white encroachment by tribes west of Fort Niagara created an emotionally charged situation during the early settlement years. In 1789, for example, Indians burned a store and killed a doctor in Canandaigua and threatened to assault settlers who were attempting to take possession of lands in New York's military tract east of Canandaigua. Phelps held a treaty with the chiefs of the Iroquois, paid them all the money he promised, and calmed the situation. But virtually all the chiefs were upset with what they felt was contempt and inferior treatment they received from the newcomers. Settlers antagonized Indians by hunting on their land, by ignoring agreements, and by acting in ways that made them appear untrustworthy. Indians then retaliated by spreading rumors of ambushes and attacks, engaging in petty thievery, and by practicing extortion in the form of threats to commit arson.[46]

It was not until American troops under General Anthony Wayne defeated a force of hostile Indians at Fallen Timbers in Ohio in 1794, and the American Congress signed a treaty with Great Britain guaranteeing British evacuation of American forts by June 1796, that Indian pressure on the settlements was relieved. With tribes calm and British evacuation assured, Indian threats to settlers became inconsequential. The Six Nations signed a Treaty of Friendship with the United States in Canandaigua in October 1794 which signified their acceptance of the results of Wayne's victory.[47] Antagonism between the two races continued, but the danger of an Indian uprising became very remote.

The threat of war with the Indians was a significant factor in deterring migration, but the resolution of this problem did not result in a rapid increase in settlements. One reason for this was the advent of a disease that pioneers called "the Genesee fever." Newcomers invariably contracted malaria, a mosquito-borne viral infection that necessitated repeated attacks before immunity developed. The early settlers called this process "seasoning," and certain potential families made up their mind that they did not want to die from either a scalping or the Genesee fever.[48]

A common description of the Genesee country as a "land of sickness and death" or as a "Valley of Bones" is probably not correct. The so-called Genesee fever, when it was uncomplicated with other diseases, was not usually fatal. But descriptions of sickness in the letters of some settlers went far to discourage eastern folk, who decided that the suffering was not worth the expected gains from a move westward. Moses Atwater, a doctor living in Canandaigua, noted that in 1795, the fever wreaked destruction from Rome to the Genesee River. "Luke Phelps has buried his wife and three of his children. One death has taken place in the Morris' family and another hourly expected. . . Life is extremely uncertain here.''[49] Settlers thus resigned themselves to living their lives in an area where periodic epidemics of fever were probable. Faith in their luck and hope of seeing better days helped encourage them to stay put.

Stress associated with the Indian threat, sickness, and loneliness brought on by prolonged separation from friends and family back east and by economic hardship produced tendencies in some people for violence or sudden flight. Canandaigua newspapers recorded the breakup of marriages, suicides, and the flight of discontented individuals. Three men, Benjamin Howell, William Cleaveland, and Thomas Hane, announced in the local paper in 1803 that their wives had suddenly run away. In that same year, Polly Dale and a Miss Bixby announced that their husbands had run off and abandoned them. Although not a regular occurrence, men and women who felt neglected, abused, or unsuccessful, turned their backs on their troubles and fled. The vast expanse of vacant territory offered an attractive opportunity to do so.[50]

Life in a growing village like Canandaigua was generally calm and geared to the rhythm of the seasons. The vast majority of settlers were law-abiding people and in tight control of their emotions. Yet the frontier life of hard work and constant struggle was no guarantee that tension and hard feelings would not erupt into conflict or produce civil disorder. The records of the General Sessions of the Peace for Ontario County, the records of the Court of Oyer and Terminer, and occasional newspaper items show that between 1794 and 1807 a total of 135 cases of crimes, ranging from assault and battery to rape, riot, and murder were presented for trial. Disputes between neighbors and conflicts between husband and wife produced a majority of the assault charges. Land boundaries, due bills, abuse of authority, and fights over women generated violence. In two cases, girl friends charged their boy friends with assault with intent to "ravish," and one was convicted.

Among personal injury crimes, riot, or brawling among men were most frequently reported. Commonly three to five men brawled and then paid fines between one dollar and six dollars each or an amount equal to two-day's to two-week's wages. Liquor was a factor in the start of many riots. Distilleries owned and operated by Oliver Phelps produced enough whisky to supply the entire region, including Fort Niagara, with as much whiskey as it could consume. In fact, drunkenness among employees endangered Phelps's merchandising business in Canandaigua. Phelps reported to his son that "Seymour is sick, Hyde has got the d—l in him—is drunk every day and pretends to be homesick. Pessley is drunk all his time. Last week a cart ran over him, now confined."[51] Phelps also reported fights and drunkenness at his distilleries where workers imbibed large quantities of the production. Nevertheless, Phelps went ahead with his whiskey making, and the courts were left with the problem of disciplining the offenders.

A type of crime with especially frightening consequence for the young community was arson. Fire was a necessity in every home, and the risk of accidental fire was always high, but arson, the deliberate effort to burn a building was of particular concern in an isolated settlement. There were five instances noted by land agents and settlers in which arson was suspected in a fire.[52]

Violent crimes like rape, murder, and arson, however, made up only 9 percent of 135 cases brought before the courts. Another type of crime—forgery, counterfeiting, and larceny—that is, crime connected with property, generated relatively few cases over a fouteen-year period. Nineteen cases were tried and eleven cases resulted in conviction. Petty and grand larceny carried stiff penalties. Fines of $5 to $25 for stealing small amounts of goods from merchants, the equivalent of about one to four week's pay for a surveyor, were levied for this offence. Grand larceny, on the other hand, carried an average sentence of three years at hard labor in state prison. In one case a man named George Dexter pleaded guilty to stealing an iron kettle from a peddler. He was sentenced to seven years in prison for the larceny of the kettle and seven additional years for the items he allegedly took from the sack. On the frontier, as in eastern communities, people believed the ownership of private property was a sacred right and not to be tampered with by those who desired to have wealth by theft.[53]

Non-criminal social problems plagued frontier outposts of civilization just as it did in eastern cities. The modern concept of welfare is very imperfectly comparable to early nineteenth-century support supervised by the overseer of the poor, an elected town official who evaluated hardship cases and spent town monies when individuals were in desperate circumstances. However, when citizens refused to aid a relative in need, the Overseer was compelled to go to court to get an order to force the person to do their duty.

Only two cases of this type were presented to the court within fourteen years. In one case, the father of a "Lame and impotent" son refused to pay anything toward his upkeep in a county alms house. The Overseer granted $9.44 a week support money to the boy and the court ordered his father to contribute 75 cents a week to the boy's support and "that he do so since he could afford it." In another case, children of "an old and impotent woman" refused to care for their mother and she became a charity case in the town of Phelps, New York. The county court again ordered that the relatives support the woman.[54]

Bastardy, another social problem that often led to the use of community funds, was not a common problem in the courts during the early years of settlement. Only five cases of this nature were presented before the General Sessions of the Peace between 1794 and 1807. Single women sued their lovers for support of a child born out of wedlock, and the court jailed the men if it determined that the offender would not pay a weekly amount, usually 75 cents, toward child support.[55]

On balance, society on the frontier during the federal era was not prone to violence, despite occasional violent incidents. The strain produced by the settling process and by isolation did cause some people to engage in drinking, fighting, and other acts of a violent nature. From the size of its population, about 18,000 by 1800, and from the number of cases presented, one can conclude that this frontier was reasonably free from internal strife.

The general friendly nature of frontier society helped integrate people coming from different economic and social backgrounds into a stratified and stable community. During early pioneering, all families were placed in the same circumstances. There were few options available to a people in need of food, shelter, and clothing. Everyone was required to dress roughly the same, eat the same food, and face the same physical and emotional hardships. "In struggling with the hardships of pioneer life," wrote Stephen Durfee, a Palmyra pioneer, "there was a fellow feeling, a sympathy for each others misfortunes. Mutual dependence made us so."[56]

During the first years social interaction between families of differing backgrounds was informal and relaxed. "If a party. . .was announced, no one stopped to inquire who were to be there, but each. . .set out for a season of general enjoyment." "There was no aristocracy in those days," remarked Mrs. Eden Foster of Batavia, New York, who, as a young girl, attended many frontier celebrations and feasts.[57] Frontier conditions made for a more interdependent and socially integrated community.

After the turn of the nineteenth century, however, a fluid frontier social structure hardened into one that was more characteristic of eastern society. When economic improvements enabled Canandaiguans to grow, economic exclusivity, social inequality, and social separation also grew. Custom tailored suits, expensive shoes, jewelry, and fancy dresses distinguished men and women whose wealth enabled them to display the material possessions that stood for social privilege. A few, including Phelps, owned slaves. In Phelps's case, he wanted to purchase black servants and did so from a person in Bath, New York, who offered him four slaves for his house.[58] The 1790 census listed eight slaves on the Phelps-Gorham Purchase and one in Canandaigua. In 1800, Canandaigua was listed as containing eight slaves, which suggests that slave ownership although a fact of daily life, was not widely practiced. In fact, Ontario County court records reveal that slaves were granted their freedom well before slavery itself was abolished in New York State in 1827.[59]

Social fragmentation was demonstrated in the formation of voluntary associations in which the members were united by a common interest. In 1803, for example, a musical association was formed in Canandaigua by individuals who enjoyed chamber music. This group sponsored recitals held in the parlors of their membership. Three years later, a private literary society was organized for the benefit of people with an interest in classical literature. Professional associations for doctors, lawyers, and businessmen were formed, and when the secret order of Masons was developed after 1790, voluntary associa-

tions constituted an assemblage of societies that together formed a powerful economic class and an elite social group which
dominated Canandaigua's society.[60]

The splintering effect of social groups and the rise of personal
wealth resulted in changes in lifestyle for many Canandaiguans.
Diet, for example, had certain social characteristics. Thus, while
all classes consumed a higher proportion of animal foods than
of vegetables, members of wealthy families had more fresh vegetables than did the poorer groups. The latter existed on salted
pork and fish and the former on beef and chicken. All classes
drank cider, rye, and corn whiskey, but the upper classes often
enjoyed wine and french brandy with dinner. Farmers made
beer to drink with their meals, while people like Phelps drank
imported champagne.[61]

Recreation and entertainment among classes also varied.
Although both rural and village folk shared common interests
in books, music, and circus entertainment, villagers tended to
enjoy dinner parties, evening musicals, and fashionable balls,
while farm folk entertained themselves with less formal events
like story telling and folk dancing. Rural entertainment was
often mingled with labor, as in corn-huskings, quilting bees, and
barn raisings, which usually ended with a great feast. On special
occasions like election day, muster day, Independence day, and
at political rallies, rural folk broke out of their routine and enjoyed a holiday from work. But the hard, monotonous work and
the miles separating small groups of settlers prevented these
people from enjoying public amusements on a regular basis.[62]

Canandaigua, a community established by investors in 1789
on the very edge of New York's western frontier, had become
by 1800 a place of extraordinary contrasts. Upwards of seventy dwellings, including many handsome residences, greeted visitors as they rode up its long, wide street to the public square.
The village was situated on a beautiful lake and appeared pro-
sperous and very stable. To a point, the facts of village life cor-
related with the visual image. Social tension existed, but it did
not overwhelm either the village or the surrounding area. The
economy was robust, thanks to new roads built to reach eastern
markets, and the settlers had emerged from the long period of
stress caused by Indian threats and by such ailments as the
Genesee fever.

Although Canandaigua was a small community planted in a forest, it was in some ways more than a simple pioneering community. Its society and social structure quietly took on the characteristics of established eastern communities. It was a community that fostered face-to-face communications on the one hand and developed clear, social divisions on the other. It was a peaceable community, but exhibited periodic outbursts of violence. The settlers did not escape such social problems as arson, larceny, rape, and welfare support by moving west. All of these problems were present in the new community.

Though individual experiences varied, the greatest gain for the settlers was economic. The promise of physical well being was often realized. At the time of the opening of the Phelps and Gorham Purchase in 1789, Phelps often wrote that these lands were among the very best lands ever available to settlers, and he was determined to make his investment and that of the settlers pay handsome dividends. Phelps's survey of townships, the layout of "city towns," the careful plan he proposed for the development of Canandaigua's main street, and the construction of an attractive courthouse added substance to his claim. Most carefully, Phelps guarded his title to all the lands he bought from the Six Nations. He knew that without a clear chain of ownership even new land became worthless. The county courthouse became the symbol of Phelps's dream by virtue of its appealing façade and the contents of its holdings. The maps, deeds, and indentures represented the property of both the expectant investors and the hopeful settlers. The frontier was a blank slate, which in Oliver Phelps's hand, became the foundation for rapid growth. The pioneers chose to live in Canandaigua because it offered a chance to enjoy many social advantages associated with life in eastern communities, and most importantly, provided a means for families to grow wealthy as the village and countryside filled with people and the land was made to yield a variety of commodities fit for human consumption.

Phelps visited Canandaigua each year during the latter part of the 1790s, and during each stay he wrote letters to his friends on the state of affairs in upstate New York. "I have dined out three or four times since I have been here at tables more elegantly spread than any I have ever seen in Connecticut," he noted in 1789. "If I owned nothing and could attend to my property in this country I should consider it worth $500,000."[63] In 1801, Phelps wrote to his son, Oliver Leicester Phelps, that he was convinced a residence in Canandaigua was appropriate. "From looking over this country. . .I am convinced it will be best for you to come into this country—everything in this quarter is in a flourishing state [and] the farmers are getting rich."[64] Exactly as Phelps had predicted in 1788, the best lands and the greatest opportunity for investment lay in the frontier lands of upstate New York.

Notes

1. Barbara Graymont, *The Iroquois in the American Revolution* (Syracuse, 1972), 262, 276–77; John A. Scott, *Fort Stanwix* (Rome, 1927), 13–16.

2. Howard L. Osgood, "The Title of the Phelps and Gorham Purchase," *Publications of the Rochester Historical Society*, 1 (Rochester, 1892), 32–33.

3. Victor S. Clark, *History of Manufacturers in the United States, 1607–1860* (Washington, 1916), 229.

4. *Letters and Other Writings of James Madison* (4 vols., Philadelphia: J. B. Lippincott and Co., 1876), I, 226–227. Cited in Curtis P. Nettles, *The Emergence of a National Economy, 1775–1815*, (New York, 1962), 78.

5. Bray Hammond, *Banks and Politics in America, from the Revolution to the Civil War* (Princeton, 1957), 53–55, 57–58.

6. Andrew C. McLaughlin, *The Confederation and the Constitution, 1783–1789* (Vol. 10 of *The American Nation*, A. B. Hart, ed., New York, 1905), 45 cited in Nettles, *The Emergence of a National Economy*, 59.

7. Oliver Phelps to Jeremiah Wadsworth, April 5, 1788, Jeremiah Wadsworth Papers, Connecticut Historical Society, Hartford, CT., Hereafter cited as JWPHC.

8. Oliver Phelps to Judah Colt, April 4, 1789, Box 2, Vol. 1, Phelps and Gorham Papers, New York State Library, Albany, NY. Hereafter cited as PGPA.

9. William Temple Franklin, *Observations on the Present Situation of Landed Property in America* (London, 1792), 12.

10. Phelps to [Anon.], August 4, 1788, Box 9, Fol. 1, PGPA. Oliver Phelps to Daniel Penfield, August 11, 1788, Box 2, Letterbook II, ibid.

11. Hezekiah Chapman to Oliver Phelps, July 11, 1792, Box 19, PGPA. Chapman reviewed with Phelps events leading to a possible purchase in 1788.

12. Chapman to William Walker, January 27, 1788, Box 1, Fol. 7, William Walker collection, Walker-Rockwell Papers, New-York Historical Society, New York. Hereafter cited as WWC.

13. Oliver Phelps to [?]. Cited in Orsamus Turner, *History of the Pioneer Settlement of Phelps and Gorham Purchase* (Rochester, 1851), 136.

14. Phelps to Nathaniel Gorham, April 22, 1788, Box 2, Letter Book II, PGPA; Phelps to Wheeling, February 26, 1788, ibid.; Turner, *Phelps and Gorham Purchase*, 137.

15. Ibid., 110–112; "Resolves of the General Court, House of Representatives, March 31, 1788." Box 1, Fol. 3, JWPHC; "Resolution and Act, Massachusetts House of Representatives, March 31, 1788," Box 1788, Phelps and Gorham Papers, Ontario County Historical Society, Canandaigua, New York. Hereafter cited as PGPC.

16. Shareholder Subscriber List, dated April 5, 1788, Box 1, Fol. 6, JWPHC.

Disposition of John Livingston, Box 84, Fol. 1, Oliver L. Phelps Collection, PGPA; Phelps to [Anon.], June 16, 1788, Box W-2, Hubbell Papers, Princeton University, New Jersey. Hereafter cited as HPP.

17. James Truslow Adams, s.v. Nathaniel Gorham, *Dictionary of American Biography*; Peter Thacher and Thomas Welsh, *Sermon on the Dead and . . . Eulogy to the Memory of the Honorable Nathaniel Gorham, Esq.* (Boston, 1796), 13–14.

18. "Gorham, Phelps and Company, Accounts with Oliver Phelps, Sale of Company Shares," Box 2, Fol. 1, Letter Book II, PGPA. "Account of the profit on one share of Genessee land, 1791." Box 2, Fol. 3, WWC.

19. Phelps to John Butler, September 1, 1790, Box W-2, HPP; "Genesee Accounts," Box 78, Fo. 2, Letter Book II, PGPA.

20. Oliver Phelps to Col. Hugh Maxwell, August 6, 1788. Box 2, Letter Book II, Ibid., Oliver Phelps to Roger Noble, August 8, 1788, Ibid.

21. Order to William Walker, August 21, 1788, Box 2, Letter Book II, PGPA.

22. Richard C. Wade, *The Urban Frontier* (Chicago, 1959), 1.

23. "Minutes of the Phelps-Gorham Company Meeting, May 6, 1789," Box W-2, HPP.

24. Ibid.

25. Phelps to Walker, October 5, 1788, Box 1, Fol. 1, WWC.

26. Minutes of the Phelps and Gorham Company Meeting, January 13, 1789, Box W-2, HPP. "Sale of land in Township 10, Range 3," Box 70, Fol. 2, Box 2, Letter Book III, PGPA. Harry J. Carman, ed., *American Husbandry* (New York, 1939), 68.

27. David. M. Ellis, *Landlords and Farmers* (Ithaca, 1946), 25–26.

28. Memorandum of Agreement, November 27, 1788, Box 1, Fol. 3, WWC; Augustus Porter, "Narrative of early years," Buffalo Historical Society *Publications* 7 (1904), 279–280; Turner, *Phelps and Gorham Purchase*, 163–164.

29. Phelps to Gorham, July 14, 1789, Box 2, Fol. 1, PGPA; "Land Sales in the Genesee," Box 2, Fol. 1, Ibid.

30. Calculation of Expenses of Purchasing the Genesee Country, Box 78, Fol. 8, Letter Book III, ibid.

31. Calculation of Expenses of Purchasing the Genesee Country, Box 78, Fol. 8, Letter Book III, PGPA; Joseph S. Davis, *Essays in the Earlier History of American Corporations* (2 vols.), Cambridge, 1917), I, 187–188; "Writs of Suit against the Bond Holders of the Phelps-Gorham Company." November 25, 1789, Box 1, Fol., 5, WWC.

32. "Petition of Phelps and Gorham to the Massachusetts General Court," February 26, 1790, Box W-2, HPP.; Benjamin Franklin Bache, *Brief of the Titles of Robert Morris to a Tract of Country in Ontario, NY* (Philadelphia, 1791), 13–14.

33. Ibid., 12–13.

34. "Account of the Profit," 1791, Box 2, Fol. 1, WWC.

35. Phelps to Theopolis Parsons, January 28, 1789, Box 2, Letter Book III, PGPA.

36. Phelps to Colt, April 4, 1789, Box 2, Fol. 1, ibid.

37. Reminiscence of Stephen Durfee cited in Turner, *Phelps and Gorham Purchase*, 283–84.

38. George S. Conover, *Canandasaga and Geneva* (Waterloo: The Waterloo Historical Society, n.d.), 124.

39. Gideon Granger to Oliver Phelps, April 9, 1802, Box 34, PGPA; Granger to Phelps, August 1, 1802, Box 35, ibid, "Newspaper Subscription List," 1810–1812, Box 88, Fol. 1, ibid.

40. "Invoice," Augustus Porter and Company, November 10, 1802, Box 1802, PGPC; Ezekiel Rogers Hyde to Oliver L. Phelps, October 16, 1802, Box 1802, ibid.

41. William H. McIntosh, *History of Ontario County, New York* (Philadelphia, 1876), 105.

42. Memorandum of Agreement, Walker and Chapin, November 23, 1788, Box 70, Fol. 2, PGPA; Agreement, Oliver Phelps and Prince Bryant, February 16, 1789, and Receipt from Phelps to Bryant, August 18, 1789, Box 87, Fol. 1, PGPA.

43. Judah Colt to Oliver Phelps, September 18, 1792, Box 19, ibid.

44. *Heads of Families*, First Census of the United States, 12 vols. (Washington, 1907–08), 7:138.

45. "Canandaigua village and farm migration patterns" cited in William H. Siles, "A Vision of Wealth: speculators and settlers in the Genesee Country of New York, 1788–1800" (Ph.D. dissertation, University of Massachusetts, Amherst, 1978), 144.

46. "Number of Indians of the 6 Nations and Distribution of Goods," November, 1792, vol. 8, Western Mementos, New-York Historical Society, New York; Gorham to Phelps, April 5, 1789, Box 2, Letter Book III, PGPA; Turner, *Phelps and Gorham's Purchase*, 143, 284–311, 315–334.

47. Ibid, 305.

48. U. P. Hedrick, *A History of Agriculture in the State of New York* (Cooperstown, N.Y., 1968), 104.

49. Moses Atwater to Oliver Phelps, September 1, 1795, Box 21, PGPA.

50. *Western Repository*, Canandaigua, New York, January 3, 1804, Ontario County Historical Society, Canandaigua, New York; Ibid., September 20, 1803; Ibid., October 11, 1803.

51. Ontario County, Ontario County Court of Sessions, Session Minutes, 1794–1806, 1 vol. Hereafter cited as S.P.'Ontario County, Sessions of the Court of Oyer and Terminer . . . , Session Minutes, 1797–1807, X vols.. Hereafter cited as O.T.' "Account of grain for the Honeoye distillery," 1802–1803, Box 1802, PGPC. Oliver Phelps to Oliver L. Phelps, January 9, 1803, Box 1803, PGPC.

52. *The People* v. *Pearson*, X, O.T. (1807).

53. *The People* v. *Dexter*, VII, O.T. (1803).

54. *Overseers of the Poor* v. *Giddings*, I S.P. (1803); *Overseers of the Poor* v. *Whitmore*, I S.P. (1805).

55. See, for example, *Overseers of the Poor* v. *Malin*, 1 S.P. (1800).

56. Reminescence of Stephen Durfee cited in Turner, *Phelps and Gorham's Purchase*, 383.

57. Reminiscence of Mrs. Eden Foster cited in Turner, *Phelps and Gorham's Purchase*, 384.

58. Agreement between Oliver Phelps and Abraham Simmonds, Contract Book, May 28, 1802, Box 93, Fol. 2, PGPA; Samuel A. Baker to Oliver Phelps, June 29, 1807, Box 44, ibid.

59. *Heads of Families*, VII, 138; Ralph V. Woods, Jr., *1800 Federal Population Census Schedule* (Cambridge, 1963), 9–13.

60. McIntosh, *History of Ontario County*, 26.

61. Edward G. Ludlow, *Observations on the Lake Fevers and Other Diseases of the Genesee Country* (New York, 1823), 26.

62. *Western Repository and Genesee Messenger*, January 24, 1804, Ontario County Historical Society, Canandaigua, New York; ibid., January 3, 1804; McIntosh, *Ontario County*, 28–29, 39.

63. Oliver Phelps to Oliver L. Phelps, November 30, 1789, Box 4, PGPA.

64. Oliver Phelps to Oliver L. Phelps, June 11, 1801, Box 5, ibid.

Index

Abel, Andries, 134
Adams, Abigail, 17
Adams, John, 8, 15, 32, 37, 40
Adams, John Quincy, 10
Adams, Samuel, 32
Addison, Joseph, 18
African Methodist Episcopal Churches, 45
Albany: as state capital, 53, 55, 109–10, 120–21; map of eastern wards of, 108; economy of, 109, 119–20; trade of, 110; celebrates New York ratification of Constitution, 110–11, 127; Antifederalist protest in, 111, 127; fire in, 111–12; slavery in, 112, 117–18; emigration to, 113, 115–17, 133; as regional center, 113; prominent residents of, 114–15; churches in, 117; free blacks in, 117–18, 122; women in, 118–19; transients in, 119–20; physical description of, 121–24, 135; shipping from on the Hudson River, 124–25, 136; roads from, 125; industrial activity in, 126–30; city government of, 128; civic improvement in, 128–29, 133, 137; enters nineteenth century, 130; antislavery views in, 134; population of, 132; mail service from to Canandaigua, 151
Albany Academy, 133
Albany County, N. Y., 103, 105–06
Albany Post Road, 125
Alburtis, Peter, 76
Alien and Sedition Acts, 85
Alsop, John, 32
Alsop, Richard, 58, 62, 78
American Bible Society, 54
American Minerva, 52

Ames, Ezra, 123
Ames, Fisher, 7
Annals of Newtown, 65
Antifederalists: in New York City, 3; in New York State, 3–4, 103, 106; in Newtown, 81–82; in Westchester County, 104–06; in Albany, 111, 127
Annapolis, Md., 2
Arnold, Benedict, 42–43
Articles of Confederation, 32, 100–03
Ash, Thomas, 52
Ash, William, 52
Atwater, Moses, 155

Bach, C. P. E., 18
Baldwin, Simeon, 135
Bancker, Evert, 116
Bank of New York, 36
Bank of North America, 141
Bank of the Manhattan Company, 47
Bank of the United States: New York Branch, 47
Bard, Samuel, 47, 51
Barry, Thomas, 133
Batterman, Christopher, 127
Battery, N. Y.: salutes from, 2, 39; Antifederalist demonstration at, 3; swimming from, 9; George Washington arrives at, 14; Alexander McGillivray visits, 19
Bay, John, 116, 133
Bay, William, 133
Bayley, Richard, 38, 47
Beekman, Cornelia, 100
Beekman, Gerard G., Jr., 100
Beekman, John J., 120

165